KAMALA DAS

A Feminist Study

KAMALA DAS
A Feminist Study

Smita Padmanabhan

Prestige
an international publishing house

Published by
Prestige Books
New Delhi
Ph. 9818755529
email: prestigebooks@gmail.com

Associate Office
60/29-45 Parramatta Road,
Concord, NSW 2137
Australia

ISBN: 81-7851-064-2

Printed at Chaman Offset Press, New Delhi 110 002

Contents

Prologue

Clearly the blue chimes in its flowing
Under my eyes;
Warmly and broadly the south winds are blowing
Over the sky.
One after another the white clouds are fleeting;
Every heart this May morning in joyance of beating
Full merrily;
Yet all things must die.

Alfred Tennyson, "All Things will Die"

Preface

The study attempts at analyzing and interpreting the English fictional works of Kamala Das in terms of her perspective about Indian society and its treatment to womanhood. The pursuit lies in exploring the diverse dilemmas, exploitation and the areas of success and defeat faced by womanhood in her constant pursuit for identity and expression, through the characters presented by Das in her English fiction. As Jane Austen says in *Persuasion*: "Men have had every advantage of us in telling their own story. Education has been theirs in so much higher degree; the pen has been in their hands." Kamala Das took it on herself to hold the pen, and let the world know the predicaments faced by woman. For accomplishing this task she employed different forms of illustration such as poems, short stories, novels, autobiography and even paintings.

Kamala Das was an epitome of the "New Indian Woman" who challenged the literary world with her writings, and boldly voiced the concerns and problems faced by the women folk. Das surpassed the "collective image" of humanity in English prose and through her characters, she powerfully presented a new genre in fiction with passionate yet compelling women protagonists. She shattered all conventions of literature and wrote unreservedly about the actualities that women faced in their day-to-day life. Her characters transcended all the barriers laid down by society and presented their hitherto unexpressed, inexpressible and taboo topics related to their mind and body. She was the pioneer woman writer, who wrote without inhibition about sex, love, exploitation and betrayal. Her radical thinking was well articulated through her characters who defied the laid down norms of society and asserted their individuality.

This work, in addition to analyzing Das's efforts in exploring Indian women's predicaments and presenting new dimensions to their individuality, aims at doing justice to her English prose works. It also aims to highlight the bold effort she made to introduce the "New Woman" image to the Indian womanhood through her women protagonists. Her literary works showcased a new breed of Indian prose, and took Indian English literature to the international levels, the proof of which came with Kamala Das's nomination for the Nobel Prize for Literature. Her writings received international acclaim but unfortunately failed to be recognized and given due credit in her own country.

I cannot close these prefatory remarks without expressing my gratitude to all those who extended their help and cooperation in preparing this project: to Kamala Das for making herself available for discussion and sharing her views and thoughts with me; to my father Lt. K. Padmanabhan, whose divine presence was constantly felt while I pursued this task, and whose dream is being fulfilled today; to my father-in-law Lt. G. Vasu, who patronized scholars and whose heavenly blessings helped me achieve this work; to my mother Mrs. Geeta, without whose inspiration and blessings I could not have done this; to my sister Soumya, and brother-in-law Deepak, whose reassurance and confidence set my spirits high and kept me, going; to my mother-in-law Smt. Savithri, on whose prayers I depended the most; to each and every member of my family whose faith and trust in my ability kept me striving for more; to my friends and colleagues for their constant support and good wishes; to Dr. Abha Pandey, English Department, Govt. Science College, Jabalpur, for all her counsel and assistance in accomplishing this work; to my husband Vijay, who kept encouraging and motivating me, never letting me surrender; to my kids, Sagar and Sania who have been pillars of my strength, putting up with me all through this period; and finally to Ms. D. Renu, Director of Prestige Books, and editors Dr. R.K. Dhawan and Dr. Suman Bala, for seeing this work through so expeditiously.

Smita Padmanabhan Vijay

Kamala Das: A Tribute

The demise of Kamala Das on 31 May 2009 took the literary world by shock. The legend has departed, but the legacy will live on. Kamala Das, popularly known as Madhavi Kutty in her native land Kerala, has left behind an enormous volume of literature that needs to be read, analyzed and meditated by every Indian. Not only have Indian women lost one of their strongest spokesperson, but also one who had spread the fragrance of Indian literature at an international level through her confessional and poignant writings. In his condolence message published in *The Hindu*, the Prime Minister of India, Manmohan Singh had the following to say: "Her achievements extended well beyond her verses of poetry. She made a mark in painting and fiction. As a syndicated columnist, her columns touched on everything from women's issues and child care to politics."

Such was the versatility of Kamala Das who thought beyond her time and lived her life on her own terms. She was and will remain to be an epitome of the bold "New Indian Woman" who had the grit to testify to the world without inhibitions, the strengths and weaknesses of both the sexes in absolute bareness and bluntness. Through her writings, she championed the cause of women's dignity and respect. She dared to tread unknown territories and delved into the unexplored. Das chose to write about issues that everyone knew but dared not discuss and her visions undoubtedly went beyond the acuity of an ordinary woman and far ahead of her time. She pursued what Vikram Seth mentioned in *The Golden Gate*.

Choose a richer lens to see with.
Reach for a vision more complete

As a writer and as an individual, Kamala Das's views were unorthodox, and it made her one of the most discussed writers in the history of Indian literature. Woman's physical and emotional expressions, in matters of sexuality, love and commitment, betrayal and extra-marital relations were the singular issues she discussed with ease and dexterity. As a maverick, she eloquently conversed about the socio-cultural landscape of Indian society, exploring daring new arenas of woman's dilemmas on sexual desires, complexities of the heart and relationships. She will undoubtedly be remembered for blatantly exposing the hypocrisy of the society's torch-bearers of equality and liberty, who found it difficult to accept her search for inner self and its expression in her writings and art in true perspective.

Sreekumar Varma in his 'Tribute' to her in the *Deccan Herald*, 6 June 2009, titled "Kamala: The Ignited Soul," writes, "When the soul ignites, words are often a balm. And from those words rise others with other words. Kamala Das inspired a young nation of poets. Her fiction too threw up several stark, aching moments."

Kamala Das was nominated for the Nobel Prize for Literature in 1984. She was conferred several prizes: the Asian Poetry Prize, the Asan World Prize, the Kerala Sahitya Akademi Award, the Ezhuthachan Award, Vayalar Award, Muttathu Varkey Award and the Kent Award. Her works have been read and translated into many languages including French, Spanish, Russian, German and Japanese.

Kamala Das experimented with all forms of art ranging from verse and fiction to drama and painting. Her popularity stood on the grounds of her honesty of expression, depth of emotions, outright narrations and her deceptive casualness in the expression of the facts of life. Kamala Das, Madhavikutty, and Kamala Suraiya, each of these names symbolized a body of her work, a phase of her life and an aspect of her personality, none of which can be obliterated by time or tide. She has made herself immortal; to borrow the lines from William Shakespeare's sonnet (18):

> But thy eternal summer shall not fade,
> Nor lose possession of that fair thou ow'st,
> Nor shall death brag thou wand'rest in his shade,
> When in eternal lines to time thou grow'st,
> So long as men can breathe or eyes can see,
> So long lives this, and this gives life to thee.

Kamala Das has left behind a legacy in Indian English literature that will be carried on by many writers and her contribution to Indian literature will keep her alive for ages to come. But what finally remains to be contemplated is whether we, as Indians could do justice to this great writer, who through her works tried to rework the thinking mentality of Indian society and model a new society where mutual acceptance and respect should be the privilege everyone enjoyed equally. R.D. Laing had commented, "Man always does not need bars of cages. Ideas can be cages too. The doors in our minds are the most difficult to open" and those were the doors which Das has tried to open and transform through her writings.

Though most of Das's writings were alarming to many in terms of its subject matter and its treatment, it was a technique that Das effectively employed to wake up the society from its slumber and ignorance. Ramesh Babu writes in *The Hindustan Times* of 1 June 2009: "She loved to shock. . . . But those who absorbed the shocks and managed to look beyond them all agreed that she was also an extraordinarily gifted writer, whose work stands at the forefront of Indian literature in two languages—English and Malayalam. Her poetry, mostly in English, has been compared to the likes of Sylvia Path and other great writers."

Kamala Das in Her Poems

Kamala Das has distinguished herself by etching a vital position in the annals of Indian English literature. Das, known for her unconventional poems celebrating revolt and forthright exploration of female sexuality, is considered as one of the pioneer Indian women writers in English who openly talked about love, lust, sexual desires and carnal experiences of women. According to her, poetry is "the April sun squeezed like an orange juice", the warmth of which gets pervaded into the mind of the readers and lingers on in their memory. The strength of her poems rests on its sensitivity, intensity, melancholy and sensuousness which arrests the reader's attention and keeps them spell-bound.

This freedom was our last strange toy.
Like the hangman's robe, even while new
It could give no pride. Nor even joy.
We kissed and we loved, all in a fury.
For another short hour or two
We went all warm and wild and lovely.   'Substitute'

A close analysis of Das's writings reveals that her poems are not the hearty and buoyant kind; instead they are tilted more towards the tragic and pessimistic side due to her early life influences and memories. Das's neglected and dejected childhood offered no sweet memories to reminisce; her early marriage to an unsympathetic and insensitive husband ruined her expectations about marriage and womanhood and her constant ill health tampered the pleasures of adulthood. All these resulted in Das remaining depressed, forcing her dreams of a blissful life to fade away in oblivion with no hopes of regeneration. The bearings of all these misfortunes of her life are manifested in her poems in some form or the other. Misery, grief, loneliness, death and disease, frustration and dejection are the overwhelming aspects dealt with in her poems that render it a melancholic vision.

Visions in Das's Poems

Das's poems are replete with a variety of visions of love, lust, sex and life; there is also the aching and breaking of heart, anger and frustration, fear and loneliness and grudge and grouse against men. Her shades of love vary from the untainted love to disillusionment in love and finally surrendering to the mystic form of love. For example, in "Love":

Until I found you,
I wrote verses, drew pictures,
And, went out with friends ·
For walks . . .
Now that I love you,
Curled like an old mongrel
My life lies, content,
In you.

But this mood of contentment in love is not very common in her poems and is quite short-lived. The swing in her mood is easily captured when we read the following lines in the poem 'A Relationship' where her bitterness towards her lovers gets visibly portrayed:

Yes,
It was my desire that made him male
And, beautiful, so that when at last we
Met, to believe that once I knew not his . . .
My body's wisdom tells and tells again
That I shall find my rest, my sleep, my peace
And even death nowhere else but here in
My betrayer's arms.

Yet another framework of love depicted in Das's love poems is the mythical love where she finally, on getting fed-up with the physical and carnal love, resorts to her quest for true love; the Radha-Krishna or the Mira-Krishna relationship. Das rises from her stupor and slumber and goes out in search of true love. In her poem "Radha," she says:

The long waiting
Had made their bond so chaste, . . .
And virgin crying
Everything in me
Is melting, even the hardness at the core
O Krishna, I am melting, melting, melting
Nothing remains but
You.

This dawning of true love is carried on and witnessed in her first poem after her conversion to Islam and dawning of a new identity. She discovers Allah as her true love and this is very forcefully articulated in her poem "Ya Allah."

The icons
have all fallen. They lie in
misshapen heaps among the bushes
that sport dusty leaves, dusty flowers.
. . . a silence shaped like paw
fallen on the city, cutting off
its breath and yet all I can think of
is my dear one's resplendent smile, he,
beloved of merciful Allah
who has unhurriedly claimed me for his own.

Das's poetry has been examined and interpreted from different angles. For instance, E.V. Ramakrishnan asserts that Das is "a confessional poet . . . she has always dealt with private humiliations and sufferings which are the stock themes of confessional poetry."[1] This opinion does find justification in most of her poems where she writes using a personal tone but what needs to be noticed is, as A.N. Dwivedi comments, "she is aware of the world around her and gives a living expression of modern Indian woman's thoughts and feelings."[2] In short, though her poems are confessional in tone they relate to the universal issues, which probably Das has herself undergone and believes women around the world also face in their everyday lives. It is this association that renders her poems the unique feeling of oneness with her readers. For instance in 'The Freak,' she writes about the hopeless and miserable condition of her love:

Who can
Help us who have lived so long
And have failed in love?

A similar expression of her loneliness and vulnerability is very poignantly brought out in "The Corridors" where Das writes:

Why do I often in
Dreams linger at strange doorways,
Lonely to the bone, feeling
Like an impostor.

Another very dominating theme is betrayal in love and marriage which is well laid out in the poem "A Relationship." In her poem "The End of Spring," Das signifies the end of the bright and hopeful season of love and the onset of the fearful and hatred:

What is the use
Of love, all this love, if all it gives is
Fear, you the fear of storms asleep in you
And me the fear of hurting you?

Her urge for independence and freedom from the clutches of unhappy relationship finds expression in "I Shall Some Day." The predicament of a wife and her maltreatment are vividly showcased in "The Sunshine Cat." The loss of love finds depiction in "The Bats":

My soul today is on its blinded, most
Frightened flight, like the bat that finds itself

In an alien zoo of light.

At the same time, the uniqueness of Kamala Das's poetry lies not just in her selection of themes but also in the volatility of her thoughts, the way they shift and assume new postures, fresh manners of defence, attack, explanation or celebration. Das's poems are entangled with the self and the wide ranging, often conflicting emotions from the yearning for security and intimacy to the assertion of the ego, self-dramatization and feelings of humiliation and depression. She has an immaculate talent to render all the different shades of emotions in one frame and express them without any perplexity. Her kind of "openness and frankness" is hardly found in any other woman writer in Indian literature. In 'The Looking Glass' one of the most intense love poems, the poet offers her readers the details of true love-making without any inhibition and distortion.

Getting a man to love you is easy
Only be honest about your wants as
Woman. Stand up nude before the glass with him.
So that he sees himself the stronger one . . .
Gift him what makes you a woman . . . and all your
endless female hungers . . . but living
Without him afterwards may have to be faced
A living without life when you move around, . . .
Body which once under his touch had gleamed
Like burnished brass, now drab and destitute.

In short we can conclude that Das's poems present women protagonists, who suffer enormously and this suffering surfaces in Das's poems in various forms. At the same time her moods have swung in all directions and she has written about things that momentarily captured her attention right from birds to seasons, children, bangles, tides and sea-shores et al. These poems illustrate the versatility of the writer and the ease and deftness with which she can write about varied topics making her a felicitous writer who is "as honest, it is as human, as she is."[3]

Das's Poems: Her Mission

Das used her poems as a means of etching a place where she could use her voice to reveal and assert herself and her feelings. Right from her first English poetry 'The Sirens,' she constantly ventured into the restricted and unclaimed territory and set a point of reference for all her contemporaries. Das through her poems opened domains, in which formerly taboo and overlooked emotions got elucidated in ways which reflected the true voice of woman's feelings and established a room for her in the literary world. Kamala Das brought into literature a sense of commitment and honesty and her poems were mostly born from personal experiences and presented without any mask.

Das was a poet of feminine yearning and her sensitivity reflected in her poems. She spoke decisively about the male dominance and oppression, within the family and society. Her poems openly discussed these issues and her concern about womankind was seen in her poems like "A Relationship," "Introduction," "Afterward" and many more. In "Afterward" Das highlights the motherly concern:

> Son of my womb,
> Ugly in loneliness.
> You walk the world's bleary eye
> Like a grit. Your cleverness
> Shall not be your doom
> As was ours.

Das talks vividly and writes invariably about the power of love and the appeal of the feminine body. Her poems more often than not, focused upon love and dealt with into the diverse facets of woman's sexual love and desires. She believed in unconditional love, and according to her, burdened love was no love at all. This stance is evidently portrayed in her poems, where she makes no effort to conceal the sensualities and eroticism that go with love and sex. She discussed her sexual triumphs and demonstrated no distress about any consequences that might result from these love affairs. She had once confessed that she "wrote the poems in the book *Summer In Calcutta* to make a man love me, to break down his resistance."[4]

The compul!sive needs of the body are expressed in an absolute matter-of-fact, no-nonsense language by Das. These find expression in the poem 'Forest Fire' where she writes as follows:

Of late I have begun to feel a hunger
To take in with greed, like a forest-fire that
Consumes, and, with each killing gains a wilder,
Brighter charm, all that comes my way. . . .
My eyes lick at you like flames, my nerves
Consume.

Kamala Das breathes an air of unconventionality and urgency. Many of Das's poems have been compared to the poems of writers like Margret Atwood and Walt Whitman. Both Das and Atwood share common moments of ecstasy in the arms of their lovers, and experience the obsessive needs of the flesh. Here is a description by Atwood who wrote the following in her moments of passion in her poem 'Variation on the Word Sleep':

I would like to follow
you up the long stairway
again and become
the boat that would row you back
carefully, a flame
in two cupped hands
    to where your body lies
    beside me, and you enter
    it as easily as breathing in
    I would like to be the air
    that inhabits you for a moment
    only.

Language and Diction

Over the years Das remained one of India's best-known women poets, widely published, extensively read, commonly discussed and greatly celebrated. Rosemary Marangoly George, an associate professor of literature at the University of California, San Diego said the following about Kamala Das, "She's always consistently being inconsistent." Das never wrote the English that others expected her to write. She wrote it as it came to her. It was an unlearnt, unkempt language which turned into magic in her hands. It was the true language of poetry and it made Kamala Das what she was, one of the finest and truest poets of her generation.

The diction of Das is typically romantic and instinctive. Simplicity and lucidity are its stamps, and is devoid of any philosophical broodings. The following lines from the poem "An Introduction," present her sense of lyricism:

> It is I who laugh, I who make love
> And the feeling shame, it is I who lie dying
> With a rattle in my throat. I am a sinner,
> I am a saint. I am the beloved and the
> Betrayed.

Her writings have lucidity of expression coupled with a tone of sincerity and straightforwardness making it comprehensible and connecting her to all her readers. She employed different devices to suit the urgency of her topic; for instance, the strategy of repetitiveness of words, phrases and expressions which made her poems poetical and appealing. A feast of musical delight is found in many of her poems as in the "The Testing of the Siren":

> Ah, why does love come to me like pain
> Again and again and again?

Das's writings by far are aphoristic as she employs abundance of imagery and symbolism which makes her poetry pictorial and sensuous. Her effective use of symbols and images reveals her artistic skills and craftsmanship. Das's writings surpassed every sphere in Indian English literature; her most remarkable achievement being the execution of her own style of English.

Her use of English vocabulary, idiom, syntactical construction also became instrumental of what lately came to be termed the 'Indianisation of English' and aided in the growth of Indian English literature; a feat of accomplishment for her which served and contributed immensely in the development of the national literature of India.

Conclusion

Though Das has only a few collections of poems to her credit, she has managed to create a place for herself and as mentioned in Geoffrey Hill's remark that the one poet who stood out in P. Lal's *Modern Indian Poetry in English: An Anthology and a Credo* (1969) was Kamala Das. Her poems as a whole are an embodiment of feminine sensibility, the hopes, fears, desires and desperations. In her poems, Das gives vent to her love and yearning to free herself from the conventions of society and live a life of fulfilment, self assertion and dignity. The woman-persona in her poetry asserts an 'indomitable will' and urges womanhood to rise above her subservient self to attain a life of satisfaction and desire. Through her poems she voices her concerns for women and their plight. In the words of Devindra Kohli, "there is something in the tone and temper of Kamala Das's work which makes one sit up from the very first poem."[5] Her collections of verse, *Summer in Calcutta* (1965), *The Descendants* (1967), *The Old Playhouse and Other Poems* (1973) *The Annamalai Poems* (1985), and lastly *Yaa Allah* (2001) have brought her worldwide recognition and secured her a significant place in the national and international literary arena.

NOTES

1. E.V. Ramakrishnan, "Kamala Das as a Confessional Poet," *JIWE*, Vol. 5 (Jan. 1977), 29.

2. A.N. Dwivedi, *Indian Poetry in English Literature: A Literary History and an Anthology* (New Delhi: Arnold Heinemann, 1983), 122.
3. Sophia Wadia, "Foreword," *Summer in Calcutta* (New Delhi: Everest Press, 1965) 7.
4. Interview by Shobha Warrior on Rediffmail.
5. Devindra Kohli, *Virgin Whiteness: The Poetry of Kamala Das* (Calcutta: Writers Workshop, 168).

Kamala Das in Her Fiction

Kamala Das, a versatile genius, whose reputation rests in her poetry, was a bilingual writer who wrote in Malayalam and English. Her themes concentrate on the pain women endure in different relationships. As T.N. Geetha puts it: "Pain resulting from loveless living, aches dulled by routine, sobs stifled by disease and death, goodness soared into harshness by callous necessity--such are the themes of her stories which have the effect of disturbing the reader's complacency and heightening the awareness of the misery around him."[1]

Her fiction deals with a variety of themes ranging from prostitution, betrayal, extra-marital affairs to child abuse and much more. Her first volume of short stories is titled *A Doll for the Child Prostitute* and the next one *Padmavati, The Harlot and Other Stories* (some of the earlier stories are reprinted in the later volume). She also has to her credit an autobiography titled *My Story* and a short novel *Alphabet of Lust*.

A revolutionary writer of stunning themes and issues, Das examines diverse ways to effectively illustrate these to the society. She herself reveals the effectiveness and benefits of the short story form, "A novelist can begin to bore the readers. Brevity is a great advantage. I like the very short one the best."[2] It is not only the theme, which is innovative but also the plot construction and techniques employed by Das, that make her stories astonishing, gripping and stimulating.

Das's themes concentrate on women-linked relationships, and she explores these from different angles. Going through her short fiction, the reader can trace the different stages of relationships in life and the various complications that go with it. The birth, growth and decay of relationships are well reflected in her stories. In her collection of stories titled *Padmavati, the Harlot and Other Stories*, seven of her short stories deal with love, marital and extra-marital relations; other five have contemplation on parent-child relationship and at the close of the spectrum of human relationship is man's alienation and existential loneliness. These are once again the bare facts of life that are presented by Das frankly and without any artifice. The lines, "Man stands alone and rotates on his own axis. Loneliness is an appendage man cannot get rid of"[3] speaks honestly about this stark fact of human life.

Her search has persistently been to establish a new class of society where there is equality of gender and women live a life of dignity and honour. The obstruction in achieving this kind of society of equals is the attitudinal factor, which plays a major role in developing man's outlook. R.D Laing comments about this: "Man always does not need bars of cages. Ideas can be cages too. The doors in our minds are the most difficult to open" [4] and these doors Das has tried to open through her writings.

Das also has exceptional capability in handling the structural form of the short story. The characteristics that Poe had laid down are followed by her in her stories. She is adept in using both the traditional and modern narrative techniques. She employs the conventional narrative technique of description, speech, report and comment in her stories and at the same time experiments in refraining from commenting about her characters.

The 'unity of impression' or 'singleness of effect' that was emphasized by Poe is found in some of her stories like 'Padmavati, the Harlot' and 'Doll for the Child Prostitute.' In these stories she has concentrated on issues of prostitution and the problems that women have to encounter. A couple of her stories like 'Lukemia' and The Tattered Blanket' have the techniques that Poe had pointed out as 'endless directedness' where the story tends to start close to the finish and is highly concentrated towards the conclusion. Another technique employed by Das to captivate her readers is the use of epiphany, whereby the writer compels the readers to self judge and assess the problems discussed in the story.

In Kamala Das's stories, the 'moment of crisis' is revealed by the change in attitude of her women characters as in 'That Woman,' 'The Sea Lounge' and 'The Kitten' etc where the protagonist undergoes change and gains a new experience. For example the mistress in 'That Woman' after her lover's death walks away from his home, as she realizes that she has no rightful place in his house. Similarly the protagonist in 'The Sea Lounge' accepts her lover's unwillingness to marry her and takes her own decision to marry her old friend who was in love with her. In 'A Little Kitten' the wife comes to know the infidelity of her husband and retaliates by being unfaithful to him.

The second story mode where a sub-plot runs parallel to the main story helps in effectively conveying Das's ideas. The second story generally runs as an undercurrent to the main story and in the words of Armine Kotin Mortimer: "The reader's role is to complete the hidden part of the story by using whatever clues the writer has given and by matching the writer's degree of cultural competence, the writer's knowledge."[5]

Das is not only brilliant in her selection of themes, but also a writer par excellence when it comes to the effective employment of various techniques of story writing, its structural management and skilful presentation. Reviewing her prose works, one can find that she carries her poetic brilliance into her prose work. Her selection of rhythm words to suit her language and style is most prominent in her story 'The Sea Lounge': "She had brought into the hotel along with her blue saris and the ring, the essence of the sea. She had become an extension of the sky, the blue sea and the sail boat." (20)

Das's amazing ability to subtly reveal multifarious facets of man and society with the simplest language of narration and style gives her stories magnificence and beauty. Her short stories with a subtle power are a class apart, and she with her prose has carved a niche in the world of fiction which is insuperable.

Though generally Das's stories are dismissed as simplistic, there is much art and craft behind their composition. The narrative techniques of Kamala Das have played a very vital role in making her stories authentic. Structurally, the stories reveal a skilful handling where brevity, comprehensiveness of matter and verbal economy resembling the verse form, make their reading arresting. Her ability to keep the story brief without much distraction and complications help to heighten and emphasize the gravity of the subject discussed. Das has struck a proper compatibility between her narration and narrative techniques. As Percy Lubbock observes: "The whole intricate question of method in the craft of fiction, I take to be governed by the question of the point of view—the question of the relation in which the narrator stands to the story."[6] Das evades giving her characters a particular name and local colouring in order to represent an entire group. This helps in suspension of our disbelief and creating a world of verisimilitude.

NOTES

1. T.N. Geetha, "Women Short Story Writers in Indian Writings in English," diss., Gulbarga University, 1998, 48.
2. An Interview with Kamala Das by T.N. Geetha, *Indian Women Novelists*, ed. R.K. Dhawan (New Delhi: Prestige, 1993), Set 2, Vol. 2.
3. Kamala Das, "Walls," 106.
4. R.D. Laing, "The Study of Family and Social Contexts," *The Study of Family and Other Essays* (Harmondsworth: Pelican, 1976) 53.
5. Armine Kotin Mortimer, "Second Stories," *Short Story Theory at a Crossroads*, ed. Susan Lohafer and Jo Ellyn Clarey (Baton Rouge: Louisiana State University Press, 1989) 278.
6. Percy Lubbock, *The Craft of Fiction* (London: Jonathan Cape, 1954) 251.

Images of Woman

Woman, Literature and Society

Literature, woman and society are three diverse, yet closely matted subjects that even the slightest variation in any one profoundly predisposes the other. The relationship between woman and literature has always been pronounced. Seema Suneel comments as follows in her book *Feminism and Literature*:

> Literature reveals principally three sets of relationships—human being in relation to the universe, individual in relation to society, and man in relation to woman . . . and reflects the various human relationships, including the image of woman and man-woman relationship.[1]

Women have since the very inception of mankind occupied the centrestage in the fictional world of letters. Women in her different forms and perspectives have adorned literature and enthralled the minds of both the writer and the reader. As Shakespeare comments in *Antony and Cleopatra*:

> Age cannot wither
> Nor custom stale her infinite variety.[2]

Literature has also played a very significant role in updating mankind by its capacity to capture and record life at different stages of time. Its ability to adapt and change with the changing age and present life, society and its people in utmost precision has always fascinated mankind. One can therefore through the study of literature unfold the past and determine the present and predict the future. In other words, literature of every nation mirrors its society and its civilization. In fact, the images, whether they are of man or woman are developed in the socio-cultural context, which has a great deal to do with the perspectives from which one observes the society. Literature can therefore be called a testimony of the happenings and developments in the society. Raymond Williams in "The Long Revolution" remarks about the relation between literature and society as follows:

> The relation between literature and society can be seen to vary considerably, in changing historical situations. As a society changes, its literature changes, though often in unexpected ways, for it is a part of social growth and not simply its reflection. At times, a rising social group will create new institutions, which, as it were, release its own writers. At other times, writers from new social groups will simply make their way into existing institutions, and work largely within their terms.[3]

Literary documentation has served as the most reliable source revealing the past with utmost accuracy. Literature in all its varied forms, has intensely human documents that have unveiled human relationships of varied kinds offering an insight into the culture of their times. Thus the changing faces of Indian womanhood down the ages can be ascertained from their reflection in the literature of the past to the present. The status of Indian woman has undergone immense transformation from the ancient Vedic era to the modern age, as depicted in the literature of the corresponding period. To get a better understanding of the present position of Indian woman and her portrayal in the contemporary Indian English literature, it is necessary to have an insight into the literature of the past and its impact on present-day woman and literature.

The status of woman underwent changes down the ages and what can finally be drawn out from the literature of the pre-Vedic to the postcolonial age is that, her position has been steadily undergoing a slow degradation process. To understand the causes that led to her present pathetic position, it is necessary to go behind the present, where lies the long-drawn-out and tangled past, out of which the present has evolved. After the Vedic age, India had a legacy of regimes and successive waves of migrations to its credit. These invasions brought with it an extremely diverse socio-cultural structure that significantly altered the Indian way of life, and consequently affected the literature also. The deteriorating status of Indian woman, which finds reflection in the various literary texts of the post-Vedic age, is a result of these changes and cultural syntheses that kept occurring so frequently in the Indian society. In brief, the changes in the society affected the position of women; literature was altered to adapt to these variations and modifications.

Woman in Indian Literature

The earliest extant Indian literature that has written records are the Vedas. Studies of these literatures reveal that during this period, both the sexes lived with mutual respect and in harmony. The most prominent literary texts of this age are the *Vedic* scriptures, the *Upanishads*, the *Epics* and Smiritis. These literatures provide ample evidence of woman as a paradigm of dignity, authority, and contentment. From the educational aspects to her marriage, the female children had equal opportunities and freedom as their male counterparts.

The most remarkable glimpses into the high status enjoyed by Indian woman are found in the Indian literature of the ancient Vedic times. The traditional Indian attitude towards women was one of veneration and esteem. How else could it be in a culture, which placed the Mother before the Father in priority for reverence? Manu the ancient lawgiver proclaimed centuries ago:

> The worth of a civilization is judged by the status it gives to its women. . . . Where women are honoured, there the gods are pleased, but where they are not honoured, no sacred rites yield rewards.[4]

An anthropological study of the Indian civilization based on the ancient Indian literature of the *Epics, Vedas*, and Scriptures, reveals that in the ancient Vedic age, both the sexes were treated with the same respect and women were given equal opportunities with men. Education, religious and societal participation, was open to her without any kind of discrimination or restriction. This impartial conduct finds mention in the Sanskrit text of Rajashekhar's *Kavyameemansa* of the Vedic age:

> *Samaskaro Atmani Samavati*
> *Na Strainam Va Purusam Va Vibhagam Apekshate.*[5]

Padmini Sengupta has written in her book *Everyday Life in Ancient India*:

> The position of women in Ancient India was free and emancipated, and women were well educated and respected members of society. A wife shared all her husband's privileges and was his common companion and helpmate in his activities.[6]

The *Rig Veda* is the first known literary treatise in which description of woman is made with great reverence. There are references of several women scholars, poets, and philosophers in the texts of *Rig Veda*, the *Upanishads*, *Ramayana*, and *Mahabharata*. There are mentions of renowned women scholars like Sulabha in the *Mahabharata* who, unable to find a suitable husband, embraced a life of studentship. *Rig Veda* speaks of marriage as a union of two equal persons of full development. Marriage though valued was not compulsory, as Will Durant remarks:

> Women enjoyed far greater freedom in the Vedic period than in later India. She had more to say in the choice of her mate than the forms of marriage might suggest. She appeared freely at feasts and dances, and joined with men in religious sacrifice. She could study, and like Gargi, engage in philosophical disputation. If she was left a widow there was no restriction upon her marriage.[7]

Family and motherhood bestowed a highly esteemed status to the woman. She retained a right over her wealth or property. Motherhood was considered the greatest glory of woman. *Matr devo bhav* is the first Upanishadic exhortation to the young, meaning, "let your mother be your God."[8] This superior position of mother finds mention even in the epic *Mahabharata*. Anees Jung quotes the words of Manu, the Hindu lawgiver in her book *Unveiling India: A Woman's Journey*:

> To be a mother, women were created and to be fathers, men. The teacher is ten times more venerable than sub-teachers; the father hundred times more than teacher but a mother a thousand times more than a father.[9]

Louis Jaccoliot's observation about Indian woman that finds mention in the book *India and Her People: 1906* is as follows, "Here is a civilization [. . .] which places the woman on a level with the man and gives her equal place in the family and in society."[10]

The Vedic society elevated woman to the level of divinity and the spiritual equality of man, as reflected in all the Indian mythological literature. Sita, Sati and Savitri are still worshipped and treated with honour and divinity. In his epic book *Return of the Aryans*, Bhagwan S. Gidwani answering the question, "Who created the Universe and who created God?" quotes Sindhuputra, the divine leader of 5000 B.C. "God created the Universe, but before Him was She—the Mother!" This reply conforms to the "Hymn of Creation," as it was then known, in Bharat Varsha and finds mention in Gidwani's book *Return of the Aryans*.[11]

All these descriptions of the literary texts lead to the conclusion that the idea of equality was most forcibly expressed during the Vedic age. These ancient books of Indian literature attest the fact without any negation that women of this age were great scholars, poets, philosophers, warriors, rulers, saints, and artists of the time. The Vedic age can thus be emblazoned as the golden era of Indian womanhood. The impression of these Vedic age women has been so great that the Sati-Savitri-Sita images and many other mythical archetypes still find mention in the modern-day Indian English literature.

In the medieval era beginning with the 13th century to the 18th century, India remained under the Muslim rulers. The condition of woman deteriorated considerably, and her status showed a striking contrast to the old. She came to be gradually considered as inferior and secondary to man. Many have called this period the 'dark age' of Indian civilization. This decline began with the Muslim invasions followed by the introduction of western ideas, which came with the British rule and brought with it more vices than good to the womanhood of India. E.A. Horowitz comments as follows in his book: "The seclusion of women in zenanas is no Hindu custom at all, but was introduced in India after Mohammedans' conquest about the time when the plantegenets rose to power in England."[12]

The loss of education paved way to illiteracy due to which the intellectual advancement of woman suffered a major setback. Thus woman lost their empowerment and became dependent on their male counterparts. This paved way to her diminishing independence and loss of self-identity, which she had been enjoying till then. The degradation process of woman being made a possession of man was a gradual one and finds mention in many literary texts. The *Maitrayani Samhita* places woman on par with dice and drink and describes her as one of the major evils in human society. Literature of the medieval age had more of men writers than women, and a negative image of woman finds portrayal in their works. Her derogatory position finds mention in the *Ramcharita Manas*, where she is grouped together with sinners, slaves and herds of animals. Tulsidas in his deservedly famous poem *The Hindi Ramayana*[13] written during Jehangir's regime, painted a picture of women, which is vilely unfair and prejudiced. Her status from the end of the Vedic age till the close of the colonial era had been a tale of steady decline and ultimate surrender and subjugation to man. By the end of this period, her status had ceased to be of an independent individual. With the turn of the century, she came to be considered as a non-existent entity and she became an appendage of men.

The society during the colonial rule had become such that suppression and violence against women had turned out to be a customary observance, and the traditions and practices that had begun during the previous age became more acute and rigid. Women's education was overlooked and domestic confinement increased. Speaking about the position of women of India, Gopalakrishna Gokhale comments as follows:

> All who know any thing about Indian women know that the turn of their mind is intensely religious . . . to their being shut out of all intellectual pursuit. And this combination of enforced ignorance . . . not only makes them willing victims of customs unjust and hurting in the highest degree but also makes them the most formidable and the most effective opponents of all attempts at change or innovation.[14]

The west too had its share of effect on the Indian minds. Influenced by the western Freudian philosophy, woman was increasingly considered merely as an object of gratification. Her status as one inferior and secondary to men had become so well established by this period of civilization that even women accepted it without any revolt. The literature of this period is replete with this secondary position specified to women. K.R.S. Iyengar states in his book *Indian Writing in English*: "Woman was easily caught in the meshes of intrigue, and social taboos of all kinds and her subservience to men gave her very little freedom of action."[15]

Except for a few examples of great women, the colonial age did not see much improvement in the women's condition and her image became very bleak around the early 19th century. It was under these conditions that the educated class of people led by Raja Rammohun Roy began the liberation activities for this suppressed class of Indian women. They sowed the seeds for her revival and gave a different direction to the understanding of the

Indian women's lives and problems. The literature of the century thus started with extensive and anxious debates about the state of women, the gender relations in Indian institution, the need to educate women to make them conscious of their rights and develop them as active participants of the country's affairs. Annie Besant advocated women's education on the ground that their progress will be a benchmark in the rise of the nation.

Influences on Indian English Literature

Literatures have always played a significant role in the lives of people, being the most powerful and characteristic form of expression of people, their life and society. Literary artists in their writings envision a world they perceive. The onset of English language in the Indian literary scenario was of an enormous aid in the revival efforts of women's condition. Literature and especially Indian English literature helped in creating a sense of awareness and in uniting people across the nations. English literature became a common platform for women worldwide to express themselves and share their problems.

The advent and growth of Indian English literature too was exploited to a great extent by Indian writers especially the women writers. Both Nehru and Gandhiji, the foremost leaders of our struggle for Independence, recognized the "language of the enemy" as an important bond not just to the wider world but also between Indians themselves. Indian English literature thus came to acquire a prestigious position in shaping the lives and thoughts of the Indian society particularly the Indian womanhood. Literature written during this period focused on the realization that depriving women education and a free growth of intellect and body, was equivalent to wasting one half of the human brainpower thereby decelerating the nation's development. Women's education and emancipation thus came to be the hub of literary debate and discussions making it an important issue of all literary works. Swami Vivekananda had propagated women's education and his opinion about the same finds expression in the following words, "Educate your women first and leave them to themselves."[16]

Authors and critics, particularly women writers, took up the deliberations about the diverse problems of women and matters concerning her exploitation and suppression by patriarchy. As Alphonso Karkala writes in his book *Indo-English Literature in the Nineteenth Century*:

> They tried to tell the world the obstacles women faced and the disadvantages they suffered in an orthodox Hindu world. These women writers struggled to give form and shape to their autobiographical accounts which attracted publishers both in India and abroad.[17]

Thus the rise and growth of Indian English writers became a decisive factor, in determining the future of the Indian womanhood. Due to lack of education, fewer women were able to employ this medium. So literature continued to remain under the domain of men, resulting in more of their outlook and concept being portrayed in the literary works. Yet it may be said that the Indian English literature since the early 19th century contributed a vital role in reviving the lost status of Indian womanhood with many male writers also taking up the women's issue in their writings. This new Indo-Anglican literature helped create awareness not only among the common public of India but also called on the attention of the world on the problems of women, creating urgency for solution. In short the prose fiction in English written by Indian writers, as H.M. Williams points out, became, "the most popular vehicle for the transmission of Indian ideas to the wider English-speaking world."[18]

Woman's Issues

According to French literary historian, M.Taine, literature is the creation of three factors: the race, the milieu, and the moment. This statement perfectly complements the Indo-Anglian literature, the renaissance of which began with Raja Rammohun Roy in the first quarter of the 19th century. It was with Roy, the pioneer of the Indian women's emancipation movement, that women's problems received a voice in literature and society. The literature of this period attempted the resurrection of the high condition of Indian women, and many of the later writers trace their lineage to him. From Raja Rammohun Roy, Bankim Chandra Chattopadhyay, the precocious Dutt sisters, Aru and Toru, Henry Derozio, Michael Madhusudan Dutt, Sarojini Naidu, Rabindranath Tagore, to R.K. Narayan, Nirad Chaudhuri, A.K. Ramanujan, G.V. Desani, Raja Rao, Mulk Raj Anand, Khushwant Singh, V.S. Naipaul, Ruth Prawer Jhabvala, Kamala Das, Shashi Deshpande, Anita Desai, Salman Rushdie, I. Allan Sealy, Arundhati Roy, *et al* there is a wide galaxy of the Indian writers in English.

The 19th century was a landmark of the beginning of an awakening period about the problems of women, revealing the hypocrisy of the traditional glorification prevalent in Indian society. Many of the writers put forth the duality of image of Indian women in their character portrayals and the contradictory reality that was prevalent. The writers painted the defied, idealized and mythical images of women to the existing debased, dishonoured, and factual status, which is her share of life in actuality. A.L. Basham comments as follows, "Woman is at once a goddess and a slave, a saint and a strumpet."[19]

Indian writing in English can be traced back to 1830s, beginning with Kashiprasad Ghosh and Derozio, the first poets writing in English. Derozio expresses his concern for *Suttee* in "The Fakir of Jungheera" (1828). He portrays the helpless predicament and exploitation of women and expresses his revolt towards this evil practice. Aurobindo Ghosh (1872-1950) had inspired many through his prose, poetry and drama. His *Savitri* is a legend; a cosmic epic and monumental edifice in the Indian lore; a masterpiece in the Indian and probably world literature.

He has made this archetype woman as wife and *Shakti*. Savitri is the *magnum opus* symbolic of the true wife's devotion and chastity with immaculate strength. Toru Dutt was the first woman poet in English (1856-1877). She was a writer who dealt with themes, which had a clear allegiance to Hindu mythology and legends. Her prose *Bianca or the Young Spanish Maiden* is a fragment of romance having a tragic plot. She had sensitive themes of women handled with care and precision and replete with all that is feminine and ingenious. Another prominent poet of the age was Sarojini Naidu (1879-1949) whose works captivated both the Indian and western audience. She added in her poetry a feminine cry to the chorus of the women's struggle for individuality.

The pioneer writers of Indian English fiction were Sochee Chunder Dutt and Bankim Chandra Chattopadhyay, whose *Rajmohan's Wife* (1864) was the first published prose. From then on, women have occupied the central theme of many literary works of the Indian English fiction. The writers have been determinedly handling themes that dealt with the deep-rooted social evils affecting the society and the problems faced by women and their exploitation. There were even in the 19th century, a handful of women prose writers, who though not much popular, did contribute to the Indian English literature in an appreciable way. These women voiced their protests through their writings, against the predicaments, struggles and sufferings of their sisters. They tried to create awareness amongst the people about the problems that the Indian women faced.

Early women writers—from Kailashbashini Debi in the 1860s to Tarabai Shinde and Pandita Ramabai in the 1880s were already identifying the distribution of power in gender relation and the subjection of women. Krupa Sattiananda (1862-1894) depicts in her work *Saguna* a young daring girl's nerve to raise her voice against the missionaries. Rockey Sakhawat Hossain (1880-1932) in *Sultana's Dream* laughs sarcastically at men by portraying a reversed status of the male community in purdah. Pandita Ramabai Saraswati (1858-1922), the most prominent writer of the age was the pioneer Indian woman who laid the foundation for women's liberation in India. In her outstanding work *The High Caste Hindu Woman*, she comments on Indian woman's submission as follows:

> When the conjugal relation is brightened by mutual love, the happy wife has nothing to complain except the absence of freedom of thought and action; but since wives have never known from the beginning what freedom is, they are well content to remain in bondage.[20]

She gives a similar description of the woman's quarters:

> Closely confined to the four walls of their house, deprived throughout their lives of the opportunity to breathe healthy fresh air, or to drink in the wholesome sunshine, they become weaker and weaker from generation to generation, their physical statures dwarfed, their spirits crushed under the weight of social prejudices and superstitions.[21]

Cornelia Sorabji (1866-1954) championed the cause of women and recorded their trials and tribulations in her book *India Calling*. The most famous internationally recognized literary figure of this age was R.N. Tagore (1861-1941) who won the Nobel Prize for his literary works. In his English fiction *The Gardener*, Tagore reveals both the male and female points of view and portrays woman as an independent being, yet totally submissive. His *Binodini* is different and has a feministic stance revealing a protesting woman. In his poem "Urvashi," he recreates the Urvashi myth.

However despite many social changes, the pre-independence Indian English literature clung to the archetypal images of Sita and Savitri. To borrow Mary Ann Ferguson's remark:

> One peculiarity of the images of women throughout history is that social stereotypes have been reinforced by archetypes. Another

> way of putting this would be to say that in every age woman has been seen primarily as mother, wife . . . their roles in relationship to men.[22]

All these writers aimed at giving a true picture of the prevailing conditions of society. Literature was thus taken up as vehicle for change and men and women contributed in their own way for the resurrection of the Indian womanhood. Though there was a difference in the depiction and interpretation of the women characters and their problems in the writings of both the sexes, their contribution is quite commendable. An analysis of some of the fictional works of men writers will be discussed in order to get a better understanding of their perspective on women and their contribution to the Indian womanhood.

Women in Indian English Fiction

The Independence movement and Gandhiji's call to women for joining hands with men in the freedom struggle came as a whirlwind and propelled Indian women out of their domestic shell into the forefront of society. R.K. Narayan, Mulk Raj Anand and Raja Rao belong to the first generation of the writers of Indian English prose who have contributed enormously to this field. Literature of this period portrays a new image of the Indian woman. Gandhiji's philosophy and his writings along with Nehru's literary works gave birth to a new culture, which stressed human values rather than religious orthodoxy. It was this outlook towards humanity presented in Bharati Sarabji's fiction *The Well of the People* (1943). The protagonist is an old widow who stands as a symbol of this new creed of humanism where there is no distinction among people. M.R. Anand (1905) has numerous novels to his credit. Some of these are *Coolie*, *Untouchable*, *The Old Woman and the Cow*, which reveal his concern for the downtrodden and underprivileged. The character of the young girl Sohini in *Untouchable* vividly portrays the society's treatment of women. She is molested by the high caste priest in spite of being an outcaste, an untouchable. In *The Old Woman and the Cow*, Anand reveals his compassion and humanity towards women. Anand renamed this novel after twenty-one years with a more appropriate title *Gauri* in which he portrays the exploitation of women by society through the persona of Gauri. The character of Gauri is a blend of Sita and Ibsen's Nora and is described as "the modern version of Sita." Anand in this novel depicts the place given to a girl child in the Indian society. Gauri is sold by her mother in lieu of the family's mortgaged land and cow. The unwilling resentful and resisting Gauri is thus forced out of her house. The novel presents the insensitivity of a society towards a woman's feelings. Anand through Gauri's character brings out the biases against women. Saros Cowasjee remarks: "Anand is deeply concerned with the social problems, and he is committed to the eradication of the evils which infest modern society."[23] Through the experiences of his protagonists, these social realities are brought to life. In the short story "Lajwanti," Anand sketches the traditional socio-cultural milieu in which women are placed.

R.K. Narayan (1906) has a wide array of women characters portrayed in his works of fiction and has a blend of both the conventional and rebellious type of characters. In *The Dark Room*, domestic disharmony is the theme of the novel. The life and misery of Savitri, the wife of Ramani, shows the hardships and mental turmoil that an Indian wife is subjected to, and how she tries to escape all this by attempting suicide. The protagonist's poignant expressions echo every Indian woman's condition:

> I don't possess anything in this world. What possession can a woman call her own except her body? Everything else that she has is her father's, her husband's, or her son's.[24]

His novel *The English Teacher* depicts the imperative part of a wife and her influence on man. The story shows the collapse and recovery of Krishnan after the death of his wife, Susheela. Krishnan who is totally devastated after his wife's death, regains normalcy only after a psychical contact is established with her spirit. Narayan thus emphasizes the vital role of a wife and her presence in a man's life through this novel. Susheela is a symbol of devoted Hindu wife who gives foremost importance to her family and domestic duty.

In another outstanding work titled *The Guide*, Narayan has sketched a very strong and forceful woman character Rosie. The neglect of Rosie by her husband Marco draws her to the tour guide Raju. She finds happiness and contentment in his company. But her love, money and fame is exploited by Raju and she finds herself betrayed by both the men in her life. Narayan depicts how society and men take every possible advantage of women and how they are exploited to fulfill their own needs.

Raja Rao, in his novels *Kanthapura*, *The Serpent and the Rope*, *The Cat and Shakespeare*, and the short stories in his *The Cow of the Barricades* restructures the mythical images of Indian women. In his fiction, he describes woman as an embodiment of the entire universe.

> Woman is Kingdom, solitude, time; woman is growth; woman is death; for it is through woman that one is born; woman rules for she is the universe.[25]

He portrays sexual and economic exploitation of the marginalized lower caste women and the poor. In *Kanthapura* (1938), women are shown as taking active part in the Freedom struggle, and society realizes the need for her participation, which finds mention as follows, "We need women in the committee, for the Congress is for the weak and the lowly."[26] However, for the female characters in Rao's stories, in spite of the death of a husband or a child, "everything went on in the household as usual." (The Little Gram Shop, 78) The short stories are deeply rooted in Brahmanism and Hinduism and Rao's eulogization of Brahmanism results in his sentimental response to the "traditional" and oppressive practices sanctified by society in the name of religion. In "Javni" and "Akkayya," Rao symbolizes the silent heroism and selfless sacrifice of Indian womanhood. Iyengar comments that woman is "the silent benefactor—'good like a cow'—of proliferating joint families."[27]

Bhabani Bhattacharya (1906) portrays his female characters with exuberance and vitality but they become victims of society's exploitation when exposed to the outer world. His characters act as a link between the old and the new, the modern and the ancient traditions. In his *Music for Mohini*, he tells the story of a city-bred girl Mohini who is married to a man with his roots in the village and the second female character is Rooplekha who is in a vice-versa situation. Both the women face problems in adjusting to their new environs and try to make the two extremes meet. They find answer to their query in accepting their roles as a link connecting two banks of a river. They consider themselves as instruments to connect cultures and different views of life and finally the women come to terms with their surroundings.

In *So Many Hungers* the writer focuses his attention on the evil practice of prostitution. Kalo, Lekha's father, is driven by hunger and to eke a livelihood, he becomes a pimp. He is shocked to find his daughter caught in one of the harlot-houses, which opens his eyes to this sordid business. He thus turns away from the work and resolves to fight against it.

Manohar Malgonkar speaks about the different shades of human relationship in his fictional works. The triumphing of Bina's love for Kiran against the severe opposing of Bina's father an influential civil servant in *Distant Drums* shows the strength of character of a woman to fight and succeed. It also depicts the extra-marital relationship between Kiran and British officer's wife, which leads to the husband's committing suicide. *Combat of Shadows* is a story of intertwining themes of love and lust, desire and aversion, and sexual attraction.

Arun Joshi's novel *The Strange Case of Billy Biswas* (1971) recounts Biswas's retreat from his wife, family and civilization and getting involved with an Adivasi girl. He has attempted to explore the depth of psyche of an individual caught in the decaying human values and his characters show a relentless search for identity and selfhood. These themes have been deftly handled in his short stories "A Trip for Mr. Lele" and "The Survivor," included in a slender volume under the title *The Survivor*.

Vikram Seth, a brilliant writer of uncanny ability, handles the important facets of life: love, marriage, man-woman relationship etc. His exploration of the issues of unhappy marital relation, broken homes, single parenthood, and divorce finds mention in his work titled *The Golden Gate*. His most popular and outstanding novel *A Suitable Boy* has marriage as its main subject. In this novel, Seth's predilection for arranged marriage is given a didactic slant by making the protagonist Lata denounce passion. This recurrent theme of renunciation of passion is Seth's motif and also has reference in his *The Golden Gate* where Liz rejects passionate love and marries a friend.

In Salman Rushdie's *Midnight's Children*, the protagonist Padma is portrayed as a 'Mother of Time' (194). Rushdie has adroitly presented through the Saleem-Padma relationship a comprehensive vision of a multi-dimensional Indian life. He uses the myth of cosmic creation to explain the process of Creation and its relation to Time. Saleem and Padma are compared to Brahma and Laxmi making the feminine-masculine polarity of a single self. Rushdie also tries to bring to light India's present, which is still held secure in mythic memories in spite of the country's advancements of democracy, voting rights for women, equal opportunities for both sexes etc. which seems to have made little impact.

The six decades of Indian independence lead us to various kinds of stocktaking. It was after the achievement of Indian Independence that the status of women came to be considered an indispensable issue and an index to measure the nation's progress. In the post-independence era, women's education had already commenced and life had started changing. It was during this period that the women's pursuit for individual status was initiated. As per the Indian constitutional laws, her status is equal to that of man, socially, economically, educationally, politically and legally. She now has the right to receive education, inherit and possess property, participate in public and political life of the nation. She has become economically independent and seeks employment and does not remain just a domestic slave. So, she is certainly enjoying an improved status now.

Undoubtedly, a vital part of these transformations has been brought about by the growth and spread of Indian English literature ever since its inception in the early nineteenth century. One of the most significant achievements was the advent of several English educated women writers into the forefront of Indian society. Their emergence into the literary scenario has been of great value. They came out of the limited world of their homes and as K.S. Ramamurti observes:

> The relief from dependence was still out of reach for most women. So the battle for emancipation was taken over by a few educated women, who in their effort to communicate to the world their own bitter experiences as women as well as their ideas of social reform, turned writers.[28]

Their remarkable contribution and authenticity in Indian English literature cannot go unnoticed and has attracted widespread attention and interest not only in India but the whole world. Indian English literature, to borrow Mulk Raj Anand's remark, "has come to stay as part of world literature."[29]

Literature is primarily motivated by various relationships that exist between individual and society and more specifically man and woman. All the major problems of women stem from diverse relationships, to which women writers have very sensitively responded in their works. Till the early 20th century quantitatively, literary writing was men's forte and had their personal outlook portrayed more prominently. The images that these male writers depicted, of the Indian women, were more according to their liking and preference. In this present era too, to some extent their image is benchmarked by the age-old ideologies, mythical images and religious beliefs prevalent in society and still greatly cherished. Women were mostly pictured as a submissive, weak and dependent being with no self-identity or self-worth.

The appearance of women writers on the scene resulted in an improved and more realistic portrayal of the womanhood and her status. Women writers took to writing about the daring issues, which were till then, taboo topics of society. Women writers made an extensive contribution in building a new position and image for Indian women. Many of them have taken up discussions about the more sensitive and intimate subject matters concerning women and their relationship with men and society. The topics they took up were very new in Indian literature, and the issues of debate were unprecedented. Prior to this, gender relations were frozen in sacred laws and customs. If they were challenged it was within the context of everyday acts of defiance by women, in their secret transgression, protest masked as sorrowful dirges and tales indicating a sense of the unfairness of the world. The covert protest was now made overtly. A qualitative leap was made away from these oblique expressions to a more open interrogation. Thus a study of these women writers of Indian English writings cannot be overlooked.

Indian women writers took up the various predicaments of women in their literary works. They probed into human relationship and crusaded against the age-old established systems. Their etching of the female characters changed quite dramatically. Shashi Deshpande is a prominent writer who has emerged in the twentieth century as a spokesperson of the Indian womanhood. Her novel *That Long Silence*, which won the Sahitya Akademi award of 1990, tells the story of an immensely tolerant Indian housewife. The protagonist Jaya represents the new image of Indian woman who tries to assert herself breaking the old norms of surrendering to the male community. In *The Dark Holds No*

Terrors, the novel ends with the central character Sarita realizing that she was actually betraying herself and with a kind of reconciliation. In her short story collections too, Shashi Deshpande focuses on women and their exploitation in different relationships and by different people. She concentrates on the theme of loneliness, defeat, guilt etc. that women experience and their suffering at the hands of society and men at large. Her stories have women who accept and come to terms with her life and situations as in "Why a Robin" and also women who are positive and strong even in the face of defeat as in "It was Dark." She has a blend of characters, some are submissive and others are rebels.

Kamala Markandaya has written several novels. Her *Nectar in a Sieve* portrays positive women characters as ideal sufferers and nurturers. Meena Shirwadkar comments:

> The cause of her suffering springs mainly from poverty and natural calamity. The women are from the rural sections of society. They are the daughters of the soil and have inherited age-old traditions which they do not question. Their courage lies in meek or at times cheerful way [sic] of facing poverty or calamity.[30]

Rukmani, the main character, and her daughter Ira suffer throughout the novel. Rukmani works hard and is devoted to her gentle husband. She endures blow after blow from life: poverty, famine, the divorce of her barren daughter, the deaths of her sons, her daughter's prostitution, and finally her husband's death. When she finds the emotional centre of her life, her relationship with her husband, threatened by the discovery that he fathered another woman's sons, she neither strikes out at him nor crumbles. Women are thus symbolized as *Shakti*, the one who has the strength to endure all difficulties with patience.

Dina Mehta in her *And Some Take a Lover* portrays through the character of Roshni the women's quest for identity. Roshni is caught in the meshes of turmoil that disturb her so much that she cannot discover or decipher her status in the society. Her lone collection of short stories, titled *The Other Woman* (1981) is about women who know their merit and do not falter to prove the validity of old values which are imposed on them, but which are easily overlooked by men. She deals with the dominance of men in the man-woman relationship where men reign supreme and they keep women in bondage. In her story "Absolution" the wife takes revenge on her adulterous husband by engaging in a similar act herself. She intentionally gives ancient mythic names to her characters like Ram and Sita to bring out a new order of the old beliefs of chastity and purity.

Attia Hossain is another prominent writer who focuses on the Muslim society and its way of life and treatment of women. Her stories underline the pain of human existence, as is evident in day-to-day events and everyday man-woman relationship. The story "The Street of the Moon" is about a beautiful young servant girl who is married off to an old opium addicted servant. Her frustration and revenge in the marriage and her husband's behaviour finds vent in her flirting with the younger men including her stepson. She runs away on being caught by her husband and ends up in a brothel where one day she is unexpectedly encountered by her husband.

Jai Nimbkar's *Temporary Answers* centres round a woman who is widowed a year after marriage. Although she agrees to live like a widow, she builds new relationships with the people with whom she works. It is a touching theme delicately handled. Her attitude is one of silent rebellion, which portrays that society still prefers to cling to the old values and resents change. At the same time there is a depiction of the gradual revolution that woman is trying to introduce into society without upsetting the old values too much.

Meera Mahadevan's *Shulamith* exemplifies the *Shakti* tradition that has the effect of showing the dominant Hindu culture upon the Jewish women of India. The novel's main character, Shulamith, experiences a "sense of dual fidelity" between her devotion to her husband and to her way of life. She chooses her way of life and remains in India when her husband leaves for Israel, but she withers away because she missies him and eventually dies as he returns. Shulamith's initially ebullient sister-in-law, Mezuzah, allowed to date and remain single, soon suffers the consequences of violating traditional Indian-Jewish mores. Influenced by Western values of romance and freedom, the young woman falls in love with a non-Jewish youth and becomes pregnant. She then experiences shame, an agonizing abortion, and a horrible marriage because her mother will not let her either marry a non-Jewish man or bring shame on the family by having a child out of wedlock. Shirwadkar explains the process that forces the Westernized young women to embrace family and tradition: "The ideas, tastes, manners adopted from the West appear to these girls attractive till some crisis or experience in their lives holds them back to the inherent culture."[31]

Mezuzah, or Maizie, becomes an image of the suffering woman: her values and personality change as she transforms first into a subdued, abused, barren wife living in poverty, then into a hard-working, self-sacrificing nurse. Shulamith appears particularly ambivalent because although Mahadevan portrays the young women Maizie and Naomi as victims of a patriarchal tradition, she makes Shulamith, who enforces social traditionalism and religious orthodoxy, a character to be highly respected. Mahadevan seems to sympathize with both sides of the conflict, but the positive image of the suffering woman remains constant. Mahadevan essentially has admiration for strong women who suffer and for younger women who learn to endure. In not being able to resolve the conflict she portrays, she returns to the traditional Sita-Savitri image.

Jhumpa Lahiri's collection of short fiction is titled *Interpreter of Maladies* (2000), which won her the international Pulitzer's prize. Her themes concentrate on infidelity in marriage, betrayal of trust, failure of communication etc. In her title story there is betrayal of trust and an extra-marital affair of Mrs. Das where she confesses to Mr. Kapasi their tour guide that one of her three children does not belong to her legal husband. There are mismatched and uncommitted marriage relations between Mrs. and Mr. Das and Mrs. and Mr. Kapasi. The infidelity in marriage is depicted in the characters of Mrs. Das and Mr. Kapasi who seem to be attracted to women outside marriage. The man-woman relationship in its sensitive aspects also finds focus in the title story "Interpreter of Maladies." Mr. Das's insensitivity towards his wife, Mr. Kapasi's sudden and temporary infatuation with Mrs. Das, and Mr. Das's friend's seduction of his friend's wife depict the frailty of commitment in relationships.

Anita Desai in her fiction criticizes traditional society, but her novel focuses on a pathetic, trapped male character whose wife despises his inability to succeed financially. Simultaneously Desai makes clear that just as the male characters are trapped in a world that offers no possibility for success, the female characters feel frustrated with a sexist society that reduces them to a dependent being clinging to men who cannot provide them with what they want. Unlike the evil Kunthi of Kamala Markandaya's *Nectar in a Sieve*, Desai's characters seem justified when they act out of self-preservation. Furthermore, unlike Markandaya's Rukmani and Ira who appear justified for their rebellion yet suffer punishment anyway, Desai's women successfully defy traditional mores. The Urdu poet's young wife in Desai's *In Custody*, who rages at her limitations and writes in her own defence, stands out as the most outrageous of these women. In fact, she radically redefines her experience by insisting on telling her story. This character's self-justification has continued in recent years as women writers tell their own stories and that of other women. When women make the lives of real women the centre of their books, they go beyond creating sympathetic female characters to making claims for an alternative reality, an alternative truth. The illicit, self-interested qualities so condemned in earlier fiction become liberating, positive, and creative forces. The pent-up psychological experiences of man are the key focus of her short stories.

Bharati Mukherjee's two anthologies of short stories, *Darkness* (1985) and *The Middleman* (1988), deal with the problems of identity crisis. Though she does not always use a woman as a centre of consciousness, yet her focus primarily lies on women. Her women protagonists are often placed in situations where they have to be effective and learn to survive in new and often hostile environments. They are finally shown to have triumphed over their situations through their strength of character. The characters of Mrs. Bhowmick and Babli in the story "A Father" depict the acceptance of the women to the western morals and life. Babli gets pregnant through artificial insemination, as she believes that her child does not need a father. The writer depicts the forceful assertiveness of identity by the women characters.

Like Bharati Mukherjee, Chitra Banerjee Divakaruni also focuses on the life of immigrants especially women. She suggests that in spite of all pains, frustrations and sufferings caused by geographical and cultural dislocation, an Indian woman's life can be a liberating influence on her. She has the strength to shed the old and begin her life afresh. Divakaruni in her stories emphasizes the importance of female sisterhood and bonding. Her collection of stories titled *Arranged Marriage* interestingly does not have a single story dealing with the subject. Arranged marriages seem to have for the writer a symbolic connotation.

Anees Jung, who first published *Unveiling India: A Woman's Journey* in 1986, also exemplifies another writer in search of new images of women. She explains the change that has taken place in Indian society so that now women can tell their own stories:

> Not long ago a woman who spoke about herself was considered a loose woman. To voice a pain, to divulge a secret, was considered sacrilege, a breach of family trust. Today, voices are raised without fear, and are heard outside the walls of homes that once kept a

> woman protected, also isolated. Some of the women who speak here have stepped out. Others who have not, are beginning to be aware, eager to find expression. But let them speak for themselves.[32]

The most recent and popular name in the list of women writers is that of the Booker Prize winner Arundhati Roy. In her book *The God of Small Things*, Ammu, Rachel, Esthapa are all portrayed craving for freedom from the male superiors. Wishing for one day, a single moment, that is free from suffering, boundaries and prejudice is their dream inverted and ultimately defeated in Roy's novel.

Images of Women in Kamala Das's Fiction

On reading the English stories of Kamala Das, a variety of woman characters can be confronted. Das presented the tumultuous emotional condition of a woman and took to revealing not only the innermost recesses of the female mind but also the injustice that was being perpetrated against women. Her autobiography *My Story* was a bold confession, a step taken to bring forth the inner turmoil that a woman faces. She voices her strong and vehement protests against the restrictions laid on woman and can be considered the instigator of a vigorous and poignant feminine confessional style of writing. In her fiction and poetic works, she has explored the feminine psyche and also the man-woman relationship and has been daring in voicing her opinions. In her collection of short stories titled *Padmavati, the Harlot and Other Stories*, she takes up the task of venturing into the uninhabited territories of man-woman relationship and deals with many bold themes of infidelity, love, sex, etc. candidly.

Das presents woman in her traditional role as caring mother as in "Moongphalli," and "Equity Shares," a loving sister as in "The Tattered Blanket," a cautious wife in "Walls" and as an understanding daughter in "Grandfather." She even portrays woman as prostitute and mistress, who accepts the contempt of society without any revolt as in "Padmavati, the Harlot" and "That Woman." Das's characters transform and grow with time and this change in woman can be observed in them. In these, women who appear to be submissive in their traditional roles voice their revolt against the injustice done to them and assert themselves when time comes. Her women are bold in making their decisions and live their lives on their own terms.

This image of Indian woman evolved by Kamala Das transcends all the barriers of culture, tradition and patriarchy. The image she presents of women personas is of restless individuals, struggling to acquire and establish a distinct identity in the traditionally male-dominated society. Das voices, through her protagonists, women's fervent protest against the absurd constraints forced on them and insists on the need of an independent individuality for the Indian womanhood. The images that Das sketches in her fiction are of radical, self-aware and self-conscious individuals sensitive about their rights. Her women personas, on realizing that they are suppressed and exploited by society, resist and fight back to affirm their identity.

Her stories are replete with this new image of Indian women who have steadily grown out of their passive acceptance of subjugation and sacrifice to an active being seeking personal gratification and self-fulfilment. The story "The Other Woman" has the image of a woman who lives life on her own terms with a married man whom she loves and does not bother about the reaction of society. When the man dies, she leaves his house without any repentance or greed for his property or money. Similarly the wife in the story "A Little Kitten" on realising the husband's infidelity retaliates in the same manner by being unfaithful to him.

Das's stories have ample evidence of such bold women characters who are strong to stand on their own and make their independent resolutions. Das also introduces women who have a broader outlook towards life like the image of the brothel owner in the story "A Doll for the Child Prostitute." Ayee is a woman who treats her girls with love and care and is also willing to accept one of them as her own daughter-in-law. Similarly there is the woman in the story "The Sea Lounge" who on being ditched by her boyfriend, is not upset; instead, accepts his decision and walks out from his life on a positive note without any despair. The woman in "The Sign of the Lion" is a woman with modern outlook and in order to fulfill her ambition in life is ready to risk her life with a man who is a womanizer. She prefers to live her present life happily and is not bothered about the future and its consequences. Das depicts diverse images of the Indian women who have shunned the conventional style of living and taken to a new outlook towards their self and their personality.

Kamala Das's Manasi, the protagonist of *Alphabet of Lust*, stands for the 'New Woman' of India. Manasi has an identity of her own and is not an appendage of the men in her life. Like Das, her women personas are also rebels and defy the traditional mores that are laid down by society to keep woman under the male dominance. Manasi who comes from a reserved and traditional background is ready to do away with her conventional lifestyle to fulfill her ambitions and wishes in life. She has no hesitation to adapt herself to a totally new atmosphere and is even willing to surrender herself to the politically powerful men to realise her wishes to gain power and money. This was a new image of woman Das introduces into Indian English literature.

These efforts to rouse the Indian women from their age-long submissiveness, inspiring them to rewrite the old norms with new ideals and principles are well depicted in Das's fiction. She encourages woman to shed inhibitions and make an effort to reveal her capabilities. She encouraged and in a way challenged Indian women to write openly about themselves, their life and problems without hesitation or inhibition. Das emphasized the importance of woman's role in redrafting her life and building a new environment for herself. Das through her writings has vehemently opposed the hierarchy of patriarchal domination and protested against the age-old acceptance of pre-established images of women in the paradigm of Sati-Savitri-Sita typecast. The images of women, as presented in her stories, are of women who are in constant search for an identity in midst of the conflict between their self and society, their inner world and external realities. Tradition and modernity are the basic type of images of women that Das has effectively and adeptly refuted.

Contention

Though the status of Indian women down the ages has kept altering but her complete emancipation is yet a distant story and no overnight solution can be anticipated. An archetypal presentation still looms large on the horizon, in spite of many changes and developments. As Meenakshi Mukherjee writes:

> One might argue that the classical ideals no longer obtain in the Indian context. But in actual literary practice, numerous characters are found to adhere to classic prototypes—especially the women of fiction who persistently enact the suffering, sacrificing role of Sita and Savitri.[33]

The facets of Indian women still find association with the mythical representation of Sita, Savitri, Shakuntala, Damayanti and Draupadi in almost every fictional form of writing. P. Lal's observations find mention in the following words: "No Indian writer in English . . . should commit pen to paper until he has spent ten years of his adult life carefully pondering the Indian classics, learning the Indian tradition, and absorbing Indian myths."[34]

Meena Shirwadkar remarks that the representation of women in Indo-Anglian literature still fulfills the ideal of suffering devotion, which she calls the *Pativrata* tradition. She argues that "a graded change" has occurred, however, in Indo-Anglian fiction. "The early novels show [the] wife in her traditional role, mainly as a house-wife and child-bearer, and the writers are preoccupied with her suffering," she claims. Later novels, in contrast, show that "the wives . . . suffer more because of the incompatibility between her individuality and awareness of herself and the traditional views of her husband and her in-laws."[35] Thus an underlying relation is still found to exist between the Indian literature of the Ancient age and the modern-day representation of women in the Indian English fiction.

So the query persists: What remarkable change in status has occurred in the lives of the Indian woman down the ages? Has her struggle taken her anywhere close to her goal of living a life of dignity and respect? Has she been able to have a place for herself in society and establish an identity of her own? Indian women still have a long way to go before achieving all this and they need to draw inspiration from Robert Frost's lines:

> The woods are lovely, dark and deep,
> But I have promises to keep,
> And miles to go before I sleep,
> And miles to go before I sleep.[36]

The role and responsibility of the women writers in creating a new pattern of living still remains to be achieved. Literature positively has a commanding role in building the Indian woman at this decisive phase where she stands at a new threshold in making an effort to redefine herself and find an independent status both in the family and society. Pam Morris explicates this point with clarity:

> It has traditionally been believed that creative forms of writing can offer special insight into human experience and sharpen our perceptions of social reality. Literary texts may therefore provide a more powerful understanding of the ways in which society works to the disadvantage of women. In addition, the strong emotional impact of imaginative writing may be brought into pay to increase indignation at gender discrimination and hence help to end it. Positive images of female experience and qualities can be used to raise women's self-esteem and lend authority to their political demands.[37]

NOTES

1. Seema Suneel, "Emergence of New Woman in Indian Fiction," *Feminism and Literature*, ed. Veena Noble Dass (New Delhi: Prestige, 1995) 219.
2. William Shakespeare, *Antony and Cleopatra*, Act II, Scene ii (London: Cambridge University Press, 1950) 235-36.
3. Raymond Williams, *The Long Revolution* (1961; Harmondsworth: Penguin, 1965) 265-69.
4. Shakuntala Rao Sastry, *Women in the Sacred Laws* (Bombay: Bharatiya Vidya Bhavan, 1960) 96.
5. Rajashekhar, *Kavyameemansa*, trans. Kedarnath Sharma (Patna: Bihar Rashtra Bhasha Parishad, 1965) 132.
6. Padmini Sengupta, *Everyday Life in Ancient India* (New York: Oxford University Press, 1950) 241.
7. Will Durant, *Story of Civilization: Our Oriental Heritage* (MFJ Books, 1935) 401.
8. *Brhad-aranyaka Upanishad* (Calcutta: Modern Art Press, 1950).
9. Anees Jung, *Unveiling India: A Woman's Journey* (New Delhi: Penguin, 1988) 68.
10. Swami Abhedananda, *India and Her People* (1906; Kessinger, 1998) 253.
11. Bhagavan S. Gidwani, *The Return of Aryans* (New Delhi: Penguin, 1994) 124.
12. E.A. Horowitz, *A Short History of Indian Literature* (London: Rare Books, 1973) 83.
13. Jawaharlal Nehru, *The Discovery of India* (New Delhi: Jawaharlal Nehru Memorial Fund, 1981) 268.
14. Gopalakrishna Gokhale, address, Conf. before the Educational Section of the Victorian Era Exhibition, London, 1897.
15. K.R.S. Iyengar, *Indian Writing in English* (New Delhi: Sterling, 1984) 437.
16. Vivekananda, *Our Women* (Calcutta: Advaita Ashram, 1982) 35.
17. Alphonso John B. Karkala, *Indo-English Literature in the Nineteenth Century* (Mysore: University of Mysore, 1970)78.
18. H.M. Williams, *Indo-Anglican Literature 1800-1970* (Madras: Orient Longman, 1976) 109.

19. A.L. Basham, *The Wonder that was India* (New York: Grove Press, 1954) 192.
20. Susie Tharu and K. Lalitha, ed., *Women Writing in India*, Vol. I (O.U.P. 1991) 247.
21. *Ibid.*, 248.
22. Mary Ann Ferguson, Comp., *Images of Women in Literature* (Boston: Houghton, Miffin, 1973) 4-5.
23. Saros Cowasjee, *Mulk Raj Anand and His Critics* (The Banasthali Patrika, Jan.1969) 58.
24. R.K. Narayan, *The Dark Room* (London: University of Chicago Press, 1981) 72.
25. Raja Rao, *The Serpent and the Rope* (London: Murray, 1960) 357.
26. Raja Rao, *Kanthapura* (New Delhi: Oxford University Press, 1989) 108.
27. K.R.S. Iyengar, 387.
28. K.S. Ramamurti, *Rise of the Indian Novel in English* (New Delhi: Sterling, 1987) 67.
29. R.S. Pathak, *Recent Indian Fiction* (New Delhi: Prestige, 1994) 11.
30. Meena Shirwadkar, *Image of Woman in the Indo-Anglian Novel* (New Delhi: Sterling, 1979) 49.
31. Shirwadkar, 49.
32. Anees Jung, 109.
33. Shanta Krishnaswamy, *Glimpses of Women in India* (New Delhi: Ashish, 1984) 370.
34. P. Lal, "Myth and the Indian Writer in English," *Aspects of Indian Writings in English*, ed. M.K. Naik (New Delhi: Macmillan, 1979) 18.
35. Meena Shirwadkar, 49.
36. Robert Frost, *Collected Poems, Prose and Plays* (New York: Library of America, 1995).
37. Pam Morris, *Literature and Feminism: An Introduction* (Oxford: Blackwell, 1993) 7.

The Feminist Approach: A Comparative Study

Feminism

Feminism is too elaborate an expression to encapsulate within a specific one-line description. In other words, it can even be said that feminism has not been defined in any precise manner. In short, feminism does not have a particular label or definition of any kind and this is well expressed by Alice Jardine in her comment:

> Who and what, then do we mean by "feminist"? That word . . . poses some serious problems. Not that we would want to end up by demanding a definition of what feminism is, and therefore, of what one must do, say, and be, if one is to acquire the epithet: dictionary meanings are suffocating, to say the least.[1]

Yet in a broadly laid perspective it is a purposely-structured stand against patriarchal exploitation of any kind and an attempt to recover a female identity and selfhood lost through time.

For a proper inference of feminism, it may be interpreted as a bid to extend membership in universal human nature, thereby gaining eligibility for human rights, to that category of 'being' named 'woman.' This is perhaps the exact point conveyed by Mary Wollstonecraft's title to her book *A Vindication of the Rights of Woman*. Feminism thus tries to establish woman as not an object or a relative entity of man, instead it categorically insists on assimilating women to the class of human race. Thus feminism claims at not differentiating woman as a separate category but in incorporating and unifying her to whatever it is to be human, women are that too, and therefore eligible for the rights that human beings are entitled for.

These and many more inscriptions have been offered as prescriptions of feminism. Some other viewpoints about feminism can also be read to get a better understanding of the feminist literature that extended and dealt with so many diverse aspects of a woman's life. According to Mary Lefkowitz, "Feminism meant equal opportunity, equal pay for equal work, recognition that a woman could do a job well as a man."[2] In the words of historian Linda Gordon, "Feminism is an analysis of women's subordination for the purpose of figuring out how to change."[3] Coming to some of the Indian writer's perspectives, Shashi Deshpande the renowned Indian fictional woman writer comments as follows:

> It took me years to say even to myself—'I am a feminist.' It was the culmination of a voyage that began within myself and went on to the ocean of women's place in the world. Today, when I call myself a feminist I believe that the female of the species has the same right to be born and survive and to fulfill herself and shape her life according to needs and potential that lies within her, as the male has.[4]

Thus the concepts of feminism are found to have different interpretations in different countries and different people like diverse feminist theory of the American, French, Canadian, African, and Indian critics. To the French women, it is greater sexual perspicuity, the American women demand enhanced political and democratic liberty, and the Indian women struggle is for equal social, economic, political and democratic independence. Elaine Showalter in her book *A Literature of Their Own* (1977) terms women's writing a "subculture" and defines the tradition by establishing three terms: "feminine," "feminist," and "female." Showalter's famous distinction states the feminine phase of internalization, the feminist phase of revolt and the female phase of self-discovery and self-recovery. Each of these phases is set to achieve greater emancipation than its forerunner, without losing its distinctiveness as women's writings.

One of the primal and seminal concerns of feminism was to declare that a woman is also a being, has an entity of her own and is not an appendage of man. The French dramatist Alexánder Dumas, the younger, was the first to use the term 'feminism' in 1872 in a pamphlet 'L'Homme-femme,' to label the then upcoming movement for women's rights. Women's demand for equality with man has been a continual theme in the western society since the past two hundred years. As early as 1777 Abigail Adams wrote to her husband John, a sitting member in the Continental Congress, admonishing him not to give such unlimited power to the husband. She commented as follows:

> Remember all men would be tyrants if they could. If particular care and attention is not paid to the ladies, we are determined to foment a rebellion, and will not hold ourselves bound by any laws in which we have no voice and representation.[5]

This concern exemplifies one of the two major precipitants of feminist sentiments in the Western world: the change in social values that justified an attempt to change social relations. The development of egalitarian values and the legitimating of insurgence that stemmed from the French and American revolutions, were used by Western women as the philosophical basis for their own insurrections. Mary Wollstonecraft wrote the first major feminist tract, *A Vindication of the Right of Woman*, in 1792 in reaction to the revolutionary French Declaration of the Rights of Man. In America the first feminist convention held in Seneca Falls, N.Y., in 1848 concluded as follows:

> He has endeavoured, in every way that he could, to destroy her confidence in her own powers, to lessen her self-respect and to make her willing to lead a dependent and abject life.[6]

Feminism in India is not just a by-product of the Western Feminist movement. Its birth in the Indian soil also credits to the dawn of an independent national identity that India obtained after her independence and the resultant new awareness, which it developed among the women folk. As Veena Noble Dass comments: "The Indian woman caught in the flux of tradition and modernity bearing the burden of the past and the aspirations of the future is the crux of feminism in Indian literature."[7]

Sushila Singh has the following interpretation, which she states in the preface to her book *Feminism and Recent Fiction in English*: "While dealing with feminism as an ideology and also as a critical tool, it is essential to take note of the fact that it assumes different configurations in accordance with racial, class and cultural variations."[8]

Feminist Literature

Feminist literature owes its rise to the desperate need of woman to make her presence and individuality felt in the society. The feminist literature attempts to set an independent paradigm of literature that expresses and explains a woman's life, her identity, her needs and aspirations, her problems and experiences from her individual viewpoint. As Sushila Singh remarks:

> As a literary discourse, it is part of the modernist search for new modes of conceptuality to change the existing pattern of gender relationship. Feminism, thus, offers a fresh perspective for critical analysis linking the study of literature with real life contexts.[9]

Till the late 19th century there was a long-standing supremacy of the male, in the world of letters. This primacy changed around the early 20th century, with the emergence of women writers, not only in India but also worldwide. Women's thoughts and dilemmas till then in the literature written by the male writers have been tantamount to masculine understanding. As mentioned in Jane Austen's novel *Persuasion*, where Elizabeth Eliot says to captain Harville: "Men have had every advantage of us in telling their own story. Education has been theirs in so much higher degree; the pen has been in their hands."[10]

As a result of this, the image of woman has been one-sided and incomplete. "In 1913 a determined and articulate new breed of women inaugurated a struggle for the liberation of women."[11] Women and their writings have made a tremendous impact in the world of literature. The literature written by these women writers cannot be captured in a simple definition. Their literature reflects many religious, historical, and cultural traditions. It includes masterpieces in many forms, particularly novels, short stories, epics, poems, drama, and essays.

Feminist literature emerged as an offshoot of the Women's Liberation Movement, and spread rapidly into diverse genres of literature of many western and non-western nations. Two hundred years back Jane Austen as a writer though very sensitive about the weakness and constraints of her sex had to restrict herself to the permissible areas of life in her writings, as a result of the then-prevalent social decorum and prudish notions. While there have been many great women, the vast majority of recorded sources were controlled by men. Their depiction in the literatures of different writers has been conditioned by the patriarchy and its social values and systems. According to Gerda Lerner in *The Creation of Patriarchy* (1986):

> Women are essential and central to creating society; they are and always have been actors and agents in history. Women have "made history," yet they have been kept from knowing their history and from interpreting history, either their own or that of men. Women have been systematically excluded from the enterprise of creating symbol systems . . . they have been excluded from theory formation.[12]

It was the need to restore woman her position in society that stirred the feminist literature to explore into the forbidden and uninhabited areas dominated till then by the male community. This effort for revival started around the 20th century with Virginia Woolf's *A Room of One's Own* (1927), French feminist Simone de Beauvoir's treatise *Le Deuxieme Sexe* (*The Second Sex*, 1949), a scholarly and passionate plea for the abolition of what she called the myth of the "eternal feminine." This seminal became a classic of feminist literature and many women writers drew inspiration from it. Other books in the line are American feminist Betty (Naomi) Friedan's *The Feminine Mystique* (1963), Kate Millett's *Sexual Politics* (1969). All these and many other feminist writers have given their viewpoints about feminism and emphasized the need for feminist literature.

Feminist movement gave impetus to widespread discontent, which finally gave rise of feminist literature. As Elaine Showalter puts it:

> It was through the women's liberation movement that we began to draw connections between our own work and our own lives, to note the disparities between the identifications and ambitions that had attracted us, along with thousands of other women, to the study and teaching of literature, and the limited and secondary roles granted to fictional heroines, women writers, or female scholars. Feminism spoke to our lived and our literary experience with the fierce urgency of a revelation or a Great Awakening.[13]

The feminist writers thus took up literature to depict the female experiences, to articulate the hidden and suppressed whimper, and in the course construct a strong platform to voice their independent opinion without fear. Juliet Mitchell commenting about the rise of women feminist writers in the English fictional scenario remarks as follows:

> Novels were written by large numbers of women. These writers were trying to establish what critics today call the 'subject in process.' What they were trying to do was to create a history from a state of flux, a flux in which they were feeling themselves in the process of becoming women within a new bourgeois society. They wrote . . . which said: 'Here we are: women. What are our lives to be about? Who are we? Domesticity, personal relations, personal intimacies, stories.[14]

Feminist theorist Jane Gallop, belatedly reading the 1972 critical anthology *Images of Women in Fiction*, registers surprise:

> It is much more diverse, sophisticated, complex, and interesting than I had imagined. Usually cited as the first phase of feminist literary study, considerations of Images of Women in literature are generally treated as juvenilia, of archival value at best . . . simpler time, when we were bold but crude.[15]

Facets of Feminism in Indian English Fiction

Coming to discuss the Indian English fiction especially those written by women writers, is found to be a combination of the "feminine" and the "feminist," making a steady effort to progressively move further close to the achievement of greater liberation and in Showalter's term become "female."

The status of the postcolonial Indian woman, and her position in the Indian society came to be much more obscure than what it had been in the past decades. The Indian woman of the new age is a beautiful smart face, burying countless anxieties and doubts. The reason for this is accounted in her breaking free from the longstanding social codes of domestic slavery and subservience, taking to active participation in the societal roles. She has finally dared to step forward from the breeder-feeder image, and venture into the diverse sectors of the male dominated public life. This stepping out from the familial life has exposed her to various threats like exploitation, sexual harassment, physical and mental abuse. As long as she obeyed the patriarchal constraints and stayed within the four walls of the house, her hardships remained limited to the household, but once she ventured out, she was compelled to counter atrocities from the outside world also. The hostile behaviour towards woman is an all-pervading element in every area where she stands equal to her male counterparts. Her apprehensions and worries, which were lately restricted to her family, have intensified with her emergence into the public life. Today she is beckoned to new challenges but with greater adversities. The modern-day woman is subjected to greater abuse, both physical and psychological from within and outside the family, than in the earlier days. Statistics show that instances of rape, molestation, eve-teasing, physical and mental ill treatment have increased. Though the Indian constitution has enacted much legislation to safeguard and protect her, she is most of the time denied justice.

Indian English feminist literature thus took up the responsibility to address all these diverse problems and issues of women in an attempt to build social revelation and seek solutions to her problems. Many women writers took up this task in earnest and have been quite successful in their endeavour. The feminist movements which began in the west, directed to the realization of the strategies used to oppress the women and keep her subservient to men. This movement guided to an urgent need to acknowledge the necessity of viewing women's problems and their needs on a wider canvas. It was this revolutionary feminist movement that led to the dawn of feminist literature. This movement did not leave the Indian women unaffected and its impact could be sensed in the writings of many of the women writers of India.

Feminist writings have a close association with the fictional genre. In the words of Sushila Singh:

> Women writers have been drawn more to fiction writing than to the other genres. . . . The very reality of woman's life situation, its "interrupted" nature, perhaps, is the reason for a close affinity between women and fiction writing.[16]

In the Indian English fiction, the women characters were influenced by the traditional images. Mythical portrayals have been an all-pervading, dominating and influential element in literature. Shirwadkar has criticized the Indian literary tradition as one overshadowed by the traditional, suffering ideal of womanhood. This representation has continued in the culture saturated by the devout portrayals of virtuous goddesses dedicated to their husbands and family. The Sita-Savitri image still exists as a powerful ideal for women in India and the Indian fiction. In the words of Meena Shirwadkar:

> Tradition, transition, and modernity are the stages through which the woman in Indo-Anglian novel is passing. The image of traditional woman, the Sita-Savitri type, was at once, easy and popular. . . . In India, with its strong bent for tradition, woman was expected mainly to live for others than for herself because "others" controlled and moulded the social structure. Even woman in life and literature herself voluntarily surrendered to the ideal of self-sacrifice. . . . Modern woman, in life, has been trying to throw off the burden of inhibitions, she has carried for ages. Yet, a woman on way [sic] to liberation, trying to be free from inhibitions, is rarely seen in Indo-Anglian literature.[17]

As new changes kept influencing society, making it alter its structure, literature too underwent modifications to meet the requirement of the time. According to the transformations in society, a graded change has occurred in the Indian English fiction and the emergence and subsequent widespread growth of feminist fiction in India owes its origin to it. It has been rightly said that the fiction written by women:

> is that creation by the woman of the woman, or by the subject who is in the process of becoming woman . . . is the prime example of the way women start to create themselves as social subjects . . . create themselves as a category: women.[18]

To understand the feminist overtures in the Indian English literature particularly the short story genre by women, the stories of three major women writers—Anita Desai, Shashi Deshpande, and Kamala Das are taken up for discussion and analysis. These women writers have dealt with and exposed through their stories diverse topics ranging from the physical to psychological aspects affecting the Indian womanhood. Their female characters stretch from women who covertly endure namelessly fulfilling the ideals of the mythical image of woman, to the modern overtly conflicting women, trying to break free from the traditional archetype. The variety and diversity that the feminine literature presents is too vast to encapsulate in a proper definition. It would be difficult to clearly differentiate and define the feminine practice of writing by the women writers. As mentioned by Helene Cixous:

> It is impossible to define a feminine practice of writing, and this is an impossibility that will again, for this practice can never be theorized, enclosed, coded—which doesn't mean that it doesn't exist.[19]

The latest developments in the Indian English fiction of the women authors is the depiction of women characters who endure endlessly fulfilling the ideals of a devout wife to women who have progressed to a conflicting yet liberated and self-aware individuals. These women writers' works have thus witnessed their incorporating experience of the two worlds, in an attempt to make a new, empowering image of women. As Anees Jung points out, "Where the two images meet lies a revelation, and a story."[20] Their stories realize both the diversity of a women and the diversity within each women. Rather than limiting the lives of women to one ideal, these writers push the ideals towards the full expression of each woman's potential.

Examining the stories of the Indian women writers, one can appreciate both the diversity of women and the diversity within each woman. The feminist movement of thoughts allowed the writers as critics to attack the meaning of sexual difference in the patriarchal ideology. Another, most recent development of the feminist view, was of an over-arching gender theory, which considers gender, both male and female, as a social construction upon biological differences. Critics of this vein found gender as imprisoning, and voiced their views against this prejudice. Images of male-wrought representation of women came under fire, prompting the emergence of a unique female consciousness and a feminist tradition in literature. To illustrate this feminist stance, Dianne Hales's comments can be quoted here:

> The goal is . . . to work towards the whole greater than its parts, that emerges when female and male join together physically, emotionally, intellectually, spiritually, sexually. Just as yin shapes yan

and day defines night, women and men are designed to complete and complement each other.[21]

Kamala Das and Her Contemporaries: The Feminist Approach:

A cursory glance into the Indian English short stories by women writers plausibly portrays the long course of journey that the feminist literature has traversed. Women are believed to be natural storytellers and the genre of short story has effectively grown in the hands of these women writers. They have engaged this form of prose fiction in revealing various predicaments of a woman's life that needs sincere examination and deciphering of the dilemmas. Reading through the short stories of Anita Desai, Kamala Das, and Shashi Deshpande the Indian women's outlook can be comprehended to a large extent.

Anita Desai, one of the most renowned Indo-Anglian women writers, with a rare verve and vigour has no parallel in Indian English fiction. She is a writer distinguished for a remarkable perceptive and sensitive exploration of the deep recesses of feminine nature and female psyche. Her themes deal psychological realism rather than social realism portraying the inner realities of woman's mind. Desai also has an essentialist approach in constructing women characters and their relation with men, and hints at the unrealized potential in men's relation to women. *Games at Twilight* (1978) and *Village by the Sea: A Long Story* (1982) are the short story collections to her credit.

Desai's short fiction is in a way, an advocacy for the legitimate rights and freedom of women and is especially noted for her sensitive portrayal of her female characters. Several of Desai's works explore tensions between family members and the alienation of middle-class women. Her forte lies in the experimentation of the psychological complexities, uncertainties of human life and concern for the emancipation of woman. Through her characters' consciousness Desai examines the same events from different points of view. Some of the author's characters are members of the Anglicized Indian bourgeoisie, whose marital problems are in the forefront. In Desai's work, her characters have often adopted an escapist way to cope with the monotonous everyday life or world outside comfortable living. Desai has commented about her work, "My novels are no reflection of Indian society, politics or character. They are my private attempt to seize upon the raw material of life."[22] Most of Desai's important representations of woman's existence, however, concern the daily lives of ordinary women in their traditional roles as wives, mothers, and widows. Although trapped in a confining society, she portrays some of her women as those who

> never lifted her voice in his presence—countless generations of Hindu womanhood behind her stood in her way, preventing her from displaying open rebellion . . . she would scream and abuse only when she was safely out of the way, preferably in the kitchen, her own domain. Her other method of defence was to go into the bedroom and snivel, refusing to speak at all, inciting their child to wail in sympathy.[23]

Desai stands out from her contemporaries for the concern she demonstrates for the characters "psychological convulsions and travails of consciousness . . . (than) the dialectic of manners and morals."[24] Even the minutest aspects of the mind and psyche are well analyzed by Anita Desai in her works. S.D. Sharma has rightly commented:

> If her novels are psychological studies on a macro level, her short stories are certainly on a micro one. If Sita, the protagonist in *Where Shall We Go This Summer?* is a psychological study on a big scale, Pat in "Scholar and Gypsy" (a famous short story) is a psychograph on a micro plane. Raman versus David, Karan versus Ravi, Monisha versus Mrs. Amul Basu are very many psychosomic character portrayals on macro versus micro levels.[25]

Desai's women are emphatic characters who try to unwind the old norms and values of patriarchy. They are the questioning kind of women who refuse to surrender timidly to the established systems of society. Her protagonists are strong-willed women who in spite of being defeated, have the guts to say "no" to society and its conventions. Anita Desai's attitude about this was voiced in an informal interview with Sujata Mukherjee on 4th April 1991, where she commented as follows:

> The characters who go against the grain of society, who try to establish as individuals, I think these are that people who interest me or excite my admiration. . . . Most of them fight against the norm, against what is expected of them. That is why a great many of them stumble and also fail. I don't think the failure is so important. It is the fight they pitch in . . . is important.[26]

Woman is not judged by her personal potential; instead, she is marked in relation with men. Her success and failures are rated in relative efficiency as a wife, mother, daughter etc. Gender relation plays a keynote role in her handling of relationships. As McClintlock comments:

> Race, gender and class are not distinct realms of experience, existing in isolation from each other; nor can they be simply yoked together retrospectively like armatures of Lego. Rather, they come into existence in and through relation to each other.[27]

Desai (borrowing a phrase Eliot used in a different context) is "a writer impossible wholly to understand and quite impossible to belittle."[28] Her stories are too complex to be judged hastily and summarily. Popular for being the pioneer of psychological paroxysm into the novels, her penchant for the same finds greater lexis in her short stories. Her title story "Games at Twilight" offers an insight into the psychology of the child. Desai confirms convincingly of her aptitude in prying into the operation of the children's mind in diverse environments. In "Studies in the Park," Desai again tries to explore into the various psychological aspects of growing up and the confusions and changes involved at different stages of life. Suno's personal disappointments vanish on seeing the old couple and the bonds of affection they share unaffected by the people around. This presents Suno, a new meaning to life. A parallel stream of thought is revealed in her novel *Where Shall We Go This Summer?* where the protagonist Sita faces a similar gloomy experience as Suno. Desai through her characters is actually advocating the need to fight back and face the adversities in life and not give up the struggle for success. An attitude to consider life as a perpetual search and not a final race is the main theory the writer advocates. A strong feminist approach supporting the initiative to revolt is found in the depiction of these characters.

In "Private Tuition" and "Sale," Anita Desai has successfully projected society and its people's attitude of thoughtlessness and disregard towards other fellow beings. This can be valued, as indirect suggestion, of a similar approach of patriarchy, towards woman and her problems, which is conveniently overlooked and purposely ignored. Another important story by Desai is "Surface Textures" dealing with Harish who shuns his responsibilities. The escapist behaviour of people finding refuge in the life of *sanyasi* is the central idea of this story. The author uses a bitter biting tone in her narration of the event. It is an outright assault on the "evasiveness and pusillanimity, cowardice and irresponsibility, of a person."[29] A reverse feeling finds illustration in the story "The Accompanist" where the character's devotion and commitment towards his master is the core subject. The author has tried to revive the old traditional sense of dedication in the guru-shishya relation, which has lost its essence, and value in the present world. A similar theme is presented in Desai's novel *In Custody* where the relationship between a poet and his admirer is explored. "A Devoted Son," "Scholar and Gipsy," and "The Farewell Party" are some of the other stories of Desai where diverse questions pertaining to man and his fight for survival in society are sketched.

Desai has a very distinctive identity specified to her women characters in her short fiction. In "Pineapple Cake," and "Private Tuition," her characters are matter-of-fact people of common life, who are far from the sophistication and refineness of behaviour. They are of the least contemplative and cultured. Mrs. Fernandez is a crude lady who savours on the pineapple cake of her taste at the wedding party rather than philosophize like her son on the demise of the gentleman who had come to attend the party. In "Private Tuition," Mrs. Bose's ill mannerism is of a great worry to Mr. Bose. She puts her husband in a precarious situation due to her uncouth behaviour and is a total failure in handling her home and children. An entirely contrasting character is exhibited in the personality of Mrs. Raman in "The Farewell Party" and Pat in "Scholar and Gipsy" and Otima Bose in "Pigeons at Daybreak." Mrs. Raman is figured as a lady of pleasing nature and pleasant disposition, who is admired and appreciated by the neighbors and friends. Pat is a lady of an independent outlook who places first her own likings and priorities in life to that of her husband and decides accordingly. She prefers a free life of her choice and detests familial bonding. Contrary to Pat is Otima Bose who values family and is a sincere and devoted wife. Anita Desai is a writer capable of bringing in the varieties of life and people and presenting them with an ease and dexterity that none can match.

Shashi Deshpande another multi-talented writer of fiction stands out for her excellent portrayals of women characters and their life. A novelist of great repute her works are inevitably woman-centric and invariably written from the women's standpoint. Like her novels, her short stories (four volumes) too have the capacity to seize the readers' interest and attention till the very finish. Concentrating more on the everyday middle-class woman, her various predicaments, and bringing forth her day-today situations are the area of expertise of Deshpande. Her protagonists are mostly women with whom her reader can well associate and readily empathize. A resolute and emphatic writer, Deshpande focuses her anger and despair at the woman's condition and through her works highlights the exploitation and victimization that women are subjected to. A popular novelist, her short fiction too has a commendable place among her literary achievements. Shashi Deshpande is an extremely sensitive writer whose passionate involvement with the women's issues finds reflection in all her fictional works. She is not a writer who is a committed feminist, but it comes to her naturally due to her sensitiveness and concern about women and their problems. She herself comments about this as follows, "Yes, I do feel that women in this country are frustrated in many ways, and that is why my characters turn out that way too. It is not intentional."[30]

The Legacy and Other Stories (1978), her first collection of short stories is replete with her expressions of feminist sentiments. In another collection titled *The Intrusion and Other Stories* (1993) all the stories except "The Last Enemy" revolve around the female protagonist. All her stories focus on women, "frustrated either sexually or professionally."[31] and their character portrayal comes to her impulsively. But she is not a creator of female heroes, instead she writes as an articulator of the suppressed Indian womanhood. Her stories are replete with Indian middle class women who "are victims of inequity: they are creatures of conventional morality: they are the ones who are unfairly abused, misused and ill-used. But they believe in conformity and compromise for the sake of the retention of domestic harmony."[32]

In the title story "The Legacy," she portrays woman's struggle for self-realization. Her deep aspiration for a child is unrealized due to her husband's sexual inadequacy. With the husband arranging for a surrogate father, her wish for a son is granted. Deshpande does not advocate this kind of bizarre sexual relations and makes her attitude clear about the moral implication of the act. "The Inner Rooms" speaks of the tragic tale of a historical character Amba forced to give up her life due to desperation and fear of ostracism from society. Through the predicament of Amba, the writer clearly depicts the hostile behaviour of society and the male chauvinistic attitude. Revolting against patriarchy would mean getting isolated, leaving suicide as the only escape route. In the story named "A Liberated Woman" the clash of male ego with a liberal female attitude is focused. The inferiority complex and prejudice of the husband is evident as he subjects his wife to sadistic torment. She confides in her friend who comments: "Surely she an educated, has no right to behave this way to plug all her escape routes herself and act like a rat in a trap." (29)

A similar note is struck in the story "I Want" and "A Day like Another," where the central characters surrender their personal wishes to that of their husband just for the sake of security and societal bonding. "The First Lady" and "Antidote to Boredom," too have the analogous theme of the acquiescence of the wives rather than revolt. The acceptance of the die-hard customs of society and their disenchantment in life cannot liberate them from the bonds of tradition and social constraints. Deshpande comments as follows to Vishwanathan: "My characters take their own ways. I've heard people saying we should have strong women characters. But my writing has to do with women as they are."[33]

We thus find that Deshpande's women characters are not deliberately portrayed as weak women, and she does not try to make her women stronger than they actually are. Instead she tries to bring forth their passivity, anxiety and struggle. G.S. Amur in his preface to *The Legacy* observes: "Woman's struggle, in the context of contemporary Indian society, to find and preserve her identity as wife, mother and most important of all, as human being is Shashi Deshpande's major concern as a creative writer and this appears in all her important stories." (10)

Shashi Deshpande has made sincere efforts in understanding the temporal truth and composite constitution of man-woman relationship. She is a staunch supporter and propeller of living and retaining relationships.

> It's needed. It's necessary for women to live within relationship. But if the rules are rigidly laid that as a wife or mother you do this or no further, then one becomes unhappy. This is what I have tried to convey in my writings. What I don't agree with is the idealization of motherhood—the false and sentimental notes that accompany it.[34]

Deshpande is excellent at tracing the tensions in which the Indian woman is caught in this transitional world. She is preoccupied with the clash between the old and the new; between idealism and pragmatism. The woman she portrays is indisputably a precursor of the 'condemned female' of modern India. Her depiction is quite unique i.e. she neither symbolizes the old, conformist image, nor a modern westernized woman. Her woman might protest, reject and resist trying to rise above the tradition but is involuntarily adapted to it. 'The Intrusion" is a story in this vein. It brilliantly portrays the story of a newly wed couple on their honeymoon trip. She reflects on their relationship where the portrayal transforms from that "of another acquiescing wife." The story is sensitively knit around the new bride with an independent outlook, who finds the idea of letting her husband whom she was "not even acquainted with . . . a month back . . . not even heard of" explore the mysteries of her body. Yet her final surrender is what she calls "his humiliation of her."

A bolder conduct of Deshpande's woman is presented in the story "The Rain" where the protagonist after some evaluation, finally defies the social constraints to start afresh a life with her previous lover. "Why a Robin" handles the theme of the woman's identity search and a confrontation with her sense of belonging. The indifference of the husband and daughter towards her fills the character with a sense of failure and guilt and she feels: "I am full of guilt these days. I am a failure . . . as wife, as a companion, as a mother. Between my husband and me there is blankness. We never quarrel. And with my daughter I am helpless." (52) Her sense of pride is hurt by the sense of isolation that she is subjected to. The estrangement between her and the other members of her family is vividly depicted in the lines: "I am an interloper. We belong to different species. I do not belong. . . . Two islands that nothing can bridge. Not the child. Not even the bridge of passion." (54). An analysis of these stories justifies what Shanta Krishnaswamy comments: "Despite the changes in the norms, the variations in taste, in standards of judgment, the impact of western culture and alien mores, economic and educational progress, she is essentially Indian in sensibility and likely to remain so."[35]

Deshpande is not one of the rebel feminists; instead she writes for the Indian woman in order to present their problems and conditions and make society aware of it. She makes it clear that "hers is not the strident and militant kind of feminism which seeks the male as the cause of all troubles."[36] Shashi Deshpande's themes are ones which deal with silence rooted in woman's relationship with her husband, children, family and society. She is very sensitive about her characters' inner psyche and all her themes are universally applicable and women can well identity themselves with her characters. Her keen and sharp insight into womanhood and her traumas has been commented on thus by Laeeq Futehally: "For me Shashi Deshpande's stories in *The Legacy* represent something about which I feel that, if only I had been more perceptive, more gifted, more imaginative, in short, if only I had been a better writer, I would have been proud to write."[37] Her own comment about her writings and her outlook about feminism is as follows:

> I write about, to be taken seriously, issues that concern all of society, and not just dismissed as 'women stuff.' Is to be a feminist to want to be like a man? I don't think so. On the contrary, to me it has meant an acceptance of my womanhood as a positive thing, not as a lack. An understanding that I am different not inferior. And how can feminism be anti-men when it is really working for a better, more meaningful and companionable relationship between men and women instead of the uneasy relationship between tyrant and oppressed?[38]

Kamala Das stands out as one of the most stupendous writers whose equal has yet to be born in Indian English literature. With a globalization of English literature, the feminist influences of the west penetrated into the Indian scenario. The pioneer of this new portrayal was indisputably Kamala Das who presented the tumultuous emotional condition of Indian woman. She pulled the screens off from the all-enduring, all-sacrificing archetype, to the more forthright and daring woman prototype. Among the feminist Indian English women writers, the highly charged confessional writings of Kamala Das are the most striking examples that remind us of great feminist writers of the west—Virginia Woolf and Sylvia Path.

Das's work in English fiction remains limited to her autobiography, a collection of short stories titled *Padmavati, the Harlot and Other Stories* and a long story *Alphabet of Lust*. Reading all her works, it can be indisputably claimed that Das, who is a downright feminist, revolts against the Indian patriarchal norms laid down for woman. Her writings have a clear portrayal of her disagreeability to submit to the old conceptions of womanhood. She is very repulsive in her depictions about the society and family's outlook about an ideal woman in her various roles of being a mother, wife, daughter etc. She blatantly hits out at social injustice and male prejudices prevalent in society and the sufferings of women under them. Exploring her works—poems, fiction, columns and autobiography—one can indisputably claim that Das's literary philosophy and perceptions were much ahead of her time. She dared to think, write and even practise in a way none other could dare.

Kamala Das is undoubtedly the spokesperson of Indian womanhood and she has always endeavoured to campaign for the emancipation of woman through her literary works. Her themes were well matched with the age and the problems that Indian womanhood was enduring under the male domination. With her realistic and confessional mode of writing, she brought into light, women's silent cry for freedom and a more humane and respectful treatment by patriarchy. She has constantly lashed out at the male ascendancy and the female oppression, both within and outside the family.

Her autobiography *My Story* is a compelling revelation of her feminity and love of womanhood. Her autobiography depicts her uncanny honesty in the exploration of a woman's body and her psyche. Das is a believer of the collective experience of the body and mind in order to make the feminity of a woman complete. A feminist writer of her repute, she has been compared with European women authors in terms of her bold and undaunted spirit in writing so explicitly and forcefully about women. Das seizes control of the society's own cultural codes, particularly those formed by religious ideologies. For example the image of Kali, in her autobiography, is absolutely amazing:

> I hung a picture of Kali on the wall of my balcony and adorned it daily with long strings of red flower, resembling the intestines of a disemboweled human being. Anyone walking along the edge of my paddy field a furlong away, could see the Goddess and the macabre splash of red. This gave villagers a fright.[39]

Similarly she uses the Radha-Krishna relationship to defend the various relations portrayed in her writings. She justifies this by saying, "I always wanted love, and if you don't get it within your home, you stray a little."[40]

Das has never associated herself with any sort of movement for fighting for the women's rights and her unconventional thoughts and beliefs find mention in her literary works. Kamala Das's short stories depict her candour in dealing with women's needs and desires both of the body and mind. Her views can be characterized as "a gut response," a reaction like her poetry, which is unfettered by other's notions of right and wrong.[41]

All her short stories have a great depth of emotion and love filled in it, and every woman can at some point or the other associate herself with its protagonist or the situations dealt with by

Das. Her contribution to the Indian English short stories, though quantitatively less, stands out by its quality. As a feminist writer, she has attempted to bring into limelight the everyday struggles and anxieties of a woman, at the same time venturing into areas unclaimed by society providing a point of reference for her contemporaries. She has transcended the role of a writer and embraced the role of a diplomat, to defend the cause of women's right to live a life of respect and dignity.

In her short story, Das discusses various issues surrounding a woman's life. Some of the very basic themes that she handles are love and lust relations found within the conventional bonds of the family and society, man-woman relationship, and woman's quest for identity. Her forte lies in the exploration of female sexuality and the importance in understanding and appreciating it. The predicaments a woman encounters in her various roles as a wife, mother, lover and daughter finds mention in some form or the other in all her stories.

Mother, sister, daughter, lover--all the numerous roles of a woman are assessed and marked by Das. The apprehensions and worries of a mother find reflection in the story "Moongphali" and "The Tattered Blanket." In the former, the mother's worry about her daughter and granddaughter's safety and security is portrayed by Das. The motherly concern and compassion, figures in the following remarks of the mother's conversation:

> I have brought with me a tin of ghee, . . . and three hundred rupees to open a post office account in our Bittu's name. . . . Times are bad, daughter, it is not right that you are left alone in the evenings. (8)

"The Tattered Blanket" illustrates the unconditional love of the mother towards her son, who though well placed in life does not bother to get even a blanket for his mother who is in need of it, instead he comes to visit her to get the share of the property. In spite of the insensitiveness and selfishness of the son towards his mother, the mother's love and concern about the son is well presented by Das.

The lustful and gripping tales of innocence and eroticism are also dealt with in a very sensitive yet compelling manner. In "A Doll for the Child Prostitute," "Padmavati the Harlot" and "The Princess of Avanti," Das adeptly deals with the burning social problems of the day like that of prostitution, rape, oppression, exploitation and brutal victimization of women and female children.

In "Padmavati, the Harlot," Das introduces to her readers Padmavati who has become a harlot to support and feed her family. She depicts the world of prostitutes and their bitter experiences from a very close quarter. Another similar touching story is "A Doll for the Child Prostitute." Both these have pictures of male autocracy over the female and the ways she is made an object of his carnal pleasure. The theme of pain is an all-pervading element in all her stories. She presents the risk of physical abuse not just of the adults but also the adolescents who are forced to enter into this work without any knowledge. The crude reality that society does not even spare small children, if they are female by sex, is well described. The juvenile prostitution is one of the major concerns of society in today's world and Das has been extremely sensitive to depict its dreadfulness and ghastliness in a very poignant manner. The snapshots of the child prostitutes and their pain in a world full of darkness, disease and death help portray the depth and seriousness of the issue. She has made the story ironic by naming all these girls after different goddesses. The pun is made at the Indian society where women are worshipped on the one hand and treated as mere instruments of sexual pleasure on the other. The ignorance and untimely maturity of children into the world of adults is well sketched in Sita's conversation with Rukmani in the story:

> "Do you think we can sleep at night in this house? We shall all be so busy entertaining the visitors."

"Visitors at night?" asked Rukmani. "Who will come at night?"

". . . Men come to do things here," said Sita. ". . . Men are real dogs." (70)

Man-woman relationship is another compelling subject handled dexterously by Das. Woman is at the receiving end of an entire social system of structure and practices based on the ideology that men are always above women in every aspect of her existence. The insensitiveness of man to understand woman's emotional and physical needs and independence as in "Sanatan Choudhuri's Wife," "Darjeeling" and "The Youngman with the Pitted Face" are issues that Das has laid stress on. Corruption of the administrative class also comes under fire. She highlights the sad plight of women and children who unfortunately become prey to the sex-trafficking and seductive roles employed by people to please the politically powerful men. Her characters like Stella, Sita, Suparna and Manasi in *Alphabet of Lust* and the maids of the Nalapat house in *My Story* strongly depict the inferior position of women in society. The treatment of woman as an object for the fulfilment of man's sexual lust and having no position of her own is skilfully sketched by Das.

She also strongly advocates the need for social restructuring and transformation in man's outlook towards woman. She also inspires women to break the old conventional norms of passivity. In *Alphabet of Lust*, Das through the character of Cyrus Contractor and Amol Mitra depicts men who are bold and independent. Through her male characters she promotes men who have the courage to introduce new concepts into society and are undeterred about the social stigmas. In her story "Moongphali," Gurucharan the peanut vendor rescues the Sikh woman, not bothered about the caste and creed issues. Again, Lachmibai agrees to marry her son to one of the prostitute girls. The two characters are representatives of change.

The themes and the message that Das's stories impart are very valid in the present day and her stories call for a sincere contemplation. Since the subject matter dealt by Das is the experience of the writer, it is authentic and convincing. If in "Iqbal" the theme of homosexuality is discussed, "Sanatan Choudhuri's Wife" has the subject of husband's suspicion about his wife. The life of an aristocratic lady is the issue debated in "Leukemia" whereas a loveless and indifferent husband is the topic of concern in "Darjeeling." The writer has undoubtedly an autobiographical element in all her works and she confesses about it in her interview with Shobha Warrior, where she comments as follows about her works:

> I certainly believe that a creator leaves a part of himself or herself in the creation. You can't escape that. You remain there, trapped within your creation and that is the most vital part in creation.

The reality of this remark is well substantiated while reading the story "A Little Kitten" which can be closely associated with the writer's personal life. In this story, the life of a couple is portrayed where mutual perfidy has become a convenient mode of living a married life of mutual non-interference by both the partners. As a writer, Das has always been sensitive about man-woman relationships and the discordant notes that are struck in living life together.

Her stories also have a wide-ranging representation of Indian woman's quest for self-assertion. The split and fractured female identity, the predicaments women face in asserting her individuality and independence, her struggle to break out of centuries of enforced subservience and silence are all emphasized in her fiction. Das who is an iconoclast uses the short fictional form in strongly presenting her views and convictions against the secondary and inferior status of women in society. She highlights the issues of sex discrimination and woman's identity and has always been a staunch advocator of equality of gender and an independent self-hood for women. Indian woman's quest for identity and its assertion has been the underlying subject in almost all her short stories. She writes with an excellent feminine sensibility and the subjects dealt with are born of her own experiences, making her a writer of felt experiences. Her stories have an urgency of expression and are confessional and genuine in its presentation and approach. They have an effusion of powerful feeling, leaving an indelible impact on the readers' mind. Das dares to present woman as a bold individual daring to break the conventions and norms of society. She presents these candidly without any apprehension or inhibition. Das in a very simple and forthright manner states the harsh naked truths. The unnamed writer of the introduction to the collection of short stories, *Padmavati the Harlot and Other Stories*, describes them as having, "a rare and adult feminism."[42] She lashes out at the meekness of the women folk and instigates them to rebel against the atrocities and discrepancies that they suffer in the male-dominated society. Das through her characters breaks the stereotype images of woman as docile and submissive with a more rebellious, dominating, assertive and forceful individuality. The nameless woman in "That Woman," "The Sea Lounge," "A Little Kitten" and "The Sign of the Lion" are clear images of the 'New Woman' concept that Das has tried to encourage. She introduces new dimension and connotation to the diverse images of woman like those of the prostitutes in "Padmavati the Harlot." She aims to establish an independent selfhood and autonomy for women and revolts against patriarchy. Das presents her women personas as dignified and confident individuals having a clear picture of their life and bold enough to make their own decisions. Extra-marital affairs, infidelity, suspicion about wife, betrayal in love and loveless marriage are the different issues debated upon in most of Das's stories and show that genuine selfless love and an authentic relationship is nearly unattainable. The presence of the supernatural and mystical experiences can also be witnessed in her fiction and autobiography.

After analyzing the stories of Das, it can be argued that her stories demonstrate a continuity of growth and development of her women characters who can be categorized on the basis of Elaine Showalter's theory. Her stories have all the three stages that Showalter describes as "feminine," "feminist" and "female." Das's "feminine" characters adorn the traditional roles of mother, wife, sister, beloved and daughter struggling to cope with their problems and dilemmas and living within the bonds of constraints and conventions like Jasmit in "Moongphali," Thangam in "Grandfather" and Padmavati in "Padmavati, the Harlot." Das also presents the "feminist" women who revolt against these traditional roles and refuse to accept the limitation of their biology as in "The Kitten," "The Man with the Pitted Face" and "Darjeeling." And finally Das has the "female" bold new women who undergo the process of self-discovery and self-revival and develop themselves as new individuals like Manasi in *Alphabet of Lust*. It has been rightly remarked about Das: "Kamala Das has more to say about the pathos of a woman emerging from a passive role to the point of discovering and asserting her individual freedom and identity."[43]

Reflections and Resolutions

A final account that can be drawn after analyzing these writers is that all of them are singular in their own individual way in asserting their feminism. Their writings have diverse contours. Anita Desai defeats the male-dominated society in the form of strong, independent, self-aware and complete characters (e.g. Bim in *Clear Light of Day*). Shashi Deshpande's protagonists are down-to-earth women aware of their existential predicament who "stoop to conquer." Kamala Das's women personas on realizing that their individuality and awareness will never be matched by man's acceptance are bold enough to defy and revolt against patriarchy and its mores. It is thus obvious from the above that women writers have in diverse ways tried to address the various issues of Indian women and render their personal viewpoints to resolve the predicaments they face. Feminism and feminist writings have thus "grown out of and built upon prevailing social needs" particularly in case of India, "where it has grown out of our own society, out of local specific issues and has addressed them directly."[44]

Indian English feminist writings have thus been emphasizing and advocating the need for women's emancipation and gender equality. These writers have addressed aspects that have been tormenting the womanhood of India right from female foeticide and equal pay to that of dowry and rape. To sum up in the words of Helene Cixous, "Almost everything is yet to be written by woman about feminity: about their sexuality, that is, its infinite and mobile complexity." (47)

A definite strategy needs to be evolved by women to negotiate and look at the world they live in with new eyes. The approach of the writers and their commitment to re-define the outlook of women will be an important index that will determine and change the future course of Indian womanhood. A determined dedication is needed to make gender equality a reality, and to achieve this according to Naomi Wolf, women should "start with the assumption that women can marshal their power and win."[45] However the evolution of feminist consciousness cannot stop at mere awareness, instead a resolution of daring and overt writings is needed to assert female self-hood. Meditating about the feminine writings of the present age, Namita Gokhale feels that through these women writers, "A new identity . . . a new credo of individuality and pragmatism is being given voice."[46]

NOTES

1. Alice Jardine, *Gynesis: Configurations of Women and Modernity* (Ithaca: Cornell University Press, 1986) 20.
2. Mary Lefkowitz, *National Review*, 11 July 1994, vol. 46, no. 13, 55.

3. Linda Gordon, qtd. Sushila Singh, ed., "Preface," *Feminism and Recent Fiction in English* (New Delhi: Prestige, 1991) 8.
4. Shashi Deshpande, "No Man is an Island," *The Sunday Times of India* (24 April 1992) 12.
5. *Collier's Dictionary* (New York: Macmillan Educational, 1986) 400.
6. *Ibid.*, 428.
7. Veena Noble Dass, ed., *Feminism and Literature* (New Delhi: Prestige, 1995) 11.
8. Sushila Singh, 8.
9. *Ibid.*
10. Jane Austen, *The Complete Works of Jane Austen* (London: Magpie).
11. Richard Marshall et al., *Great Events of the 20th Century: How They Changed Our Lives* (New York; Dai Nippon, 1977) 76.
12. Gerda Lerner, *The Creation of Patriarchy* (London: Oxford University Press, 1986) 5.
13. Elaine Showalter, ed., *The New Feminist Criticism: Essays on Women, Literature and Theory* (New York: Pantheon, 1985) 5.
14. Juliet Mitchell, "Femininity, Narrative and Psychoanalysis," *Women: The Longest Revolution* (London: Penguin, 1984) 427.
15. Jane Gallop, *Around 1981* (New York: Routledge, 1991) 79.
16. Sushila Singh, 8.
17. Meena Shirwadkar, *Image of Woman in the Indo-Anglian Novel* (New Delhi: Sterling, 1979) 153-54.
18. Mitchell, 427.
19. Helene Cixous, "The Laugh of Medusa," trans. Keith Cohen and Paula Cohen, *New French Feminism*, ed. Elaine Marks (New York: Schockin, 1981) 243.
20. Anees Jung, *Unveiling India: A Woman's Journey* (New Delhi: Penguin, 1988).
21. Dianne Hales, *Just Like a Woman* (New York: Bantam, 1999).
22. Anita Desai, "An interview with Anita Desai" by Yashodhara Dalmia, *The Times of India*.
23. Anita Desai, *In Custody* (London: Heinemann, 1984) 146.
24. T.N. Geetha, "Women Short Story Writers in Indian Writing in English," diss. (Gulbarga University, 1989) 48.
25. S.D. Sharma, "Anita Desai," *Studies in Contemporary Indian-English Short Stories*, ed. A.N. Dwivedi, 26.

26. Qtd. "Anita Desai's Major Women Characters," *Indian Writing Today*, ed. C.R. Visweswara Rao (New Delhi: Prestige, 1996) 114.
27. McClintlock Anne, *Imperial Leather: Race, Gender, and Sexuality in the Colonial Context* (New York; Routledge, 1995).
28. Qtd. Walter Allen, *The Short Story in English* (Oxford: Clarendon Press, 1981) 10.
29. S.D. Sharma, 28.
30. M.D. Riti, Interview 'There is no looking back for Shashi Deshpande' *Eve's Weekly* (18-24 June, 1988) 28.
31. *Ibid.*, 28.
32. Laeeq Futehally, rev. of *The Legacy*, *Indian Book Chronicle*, Jan. 1982: 24.
33. Vimala, 'Interview with Shashi Deshpande" *Literature Alive*, (Dec.1987) 12.
34. Vishwanathan, 12
35. Shanta Krishnaswamy, *The Woman in Indian Fiction in English* (New Delhi: Ashish, 1984) 50.
36. Sarabjit K. Sandhu, *The Image of Woman in the Novels of Shashi Deshpande* (New Delhi: Prestige, 1991) 14.
37. Laeeq Futehally, 24.
38. Shashi Deshpande, "No Man is an Island" *The Sunday Times of India* (24 April 1992) 12.
39. *My Story*, 201
40. In an interview with Shobha Warrior, Rediffmail.com.
41. P.P. Raveendran, "Text as History, History as Text: A Reading of Kamala Das's Annamalai Poems." *Journal of Commonwealth Literature*, 1994: 47-54.
42. Kamala Das, *Padmavati, the Harlot and Other Stories* (New Delhi: Sterling Paperbacks, 1994) 5.
43. Devendra Kohli, *Kamala Das* (New Delhi: Arnold-Heinemann, 1975) 29.
44. Shashi Deshpande, "No Man is an Island."
45. Naomi Wolf, *Fire with Fire: The New Female Power and How it Will Change the 21st Century* (Chatto and Windus: London, 1993) 179.
46. Namita Gokhale, "Women Writers Shape Their Own Destiny," *The Hindu*, 7 July 1996: 3.

Woman's Quest for Identity and Its Assertion

Identity Quest: The Term and its Implications

"Know thyself," said Socrates.[1] To 'know thyself,' as he put it, is both a fundamental human urge and a basic question in philosophy. A little self-knowledge and having some idea of who or what one is, help to determine how we ought to live and conduct ourselves. Most of the people do not know about themselves, instead carry a romanticized conception of their self. They either adhere to an imagined inheritance, or subscribe to safeguarding societies' longstanding static attitude about an individual's personality. In short, they are ready to sacrifice anything to save some essence of the idealized identity. There are others who abandon the old notion of a conventional or fixed identity and adorn themselves with new and challenging individuality, understanding and adapting to the changing needs of time. It is this quest for a revolution in identity, which is quite relevant in the case of the modern-day woman. As per the dictionary:

> Identity is one's sense of being distinguishable from other persons; or being who or what one is.[2]
>
> Quest means search or pursuit made in order to secure an object or achieve a goal.[3]

The issue of women's quest for identity is being contested in the literary arena not only in India but also worldwide and self-awareness and self-assertiveness is being challenged. Woman has strongly and overtly started reacting to her age-old secondary position to man and her suppression by patriarchy. On the entrapment of woman, John Stuart Mill remarks: "Women are brought up from earliest years . . . to live for others, to make a complete negation of themselves and to have no life but in their affections."[4]

Women writers have seriously taken up a search for their selfhood essentially in an attempt to find an answer to the suppressive, subjective and secondary attitude that is meted out to the women folk by patriarchy. This pursuit is explicitly portrayed in the post-Independence literature of woman writers. The spread and growth of Indian English literature created a better intellectual understanding among the womanhood resulting in the disintegration of the old norms of female subjugation and subservience. Complemented with the advent and spread of the women's liberation movement along with the successful burgeoning of feminist literature, saw the birth to a new sense of consciousness and dynamism in the women writing. From this arouse new problems and new attempts at solution. The major issue, which came to light, was that concerning the Indian womanhood and her identity. In the words of Veena Noble Dass: "A search for identity and a quest for the definition of the self have become the prime features of women in literature under the sway of feminism. And so one of the major issues . . . recurrently dealt with by feminist writers is the identity crisis."[5]

The issues of identity are far-ranging and it would be absurd to assume that all of it could be covered at a stretch. Rather, the women depicted in the English fiction of few feminist writers and in the short stories of Kamala Das have been chosen as a platform to understand the different issues of women. The study attempts to at least scratch the surface of the problem, which has long bewildered the modern-day Indian women.

A mystified and uncertain feeling of who or what she is has led womanhood to an identity crisis. The diverse issues of her identity include false identity moulded through social status, identity amidst an uncaring environment, racial identity and the irrationality of male chauvinism, mythical relation and identity, integrity and identity, and finally changing personal values and identity. Consequently woman passed through a phase what Erickson termed as 'identity crisis.'[6] It was this prevailing problem of an undefined, unascertained identity that led womanhood in quest of an appropriate solution to resolve their identity crisis. Women's personality had always remained blurred and eclipsed, presenting an undefined picture of her true individuality and worth. The 20th century witnessed a shift in values and outlook and these changes have been reflected in the literature of the age also.

This 'identity crisis' can be discerned if one compares the images of suffering women in Kamala Markandaya's and Meera Mahadevan's fictional works to the recent subversions and expansions of traditional images in the works of Kamala Das, Anita Desai and Shobha De. Comparing the women characters of Markandaya and Mahadevan to those of Desai, Das and De, it can be well perceived that the women protagonists of the latter assert themselves more strongly and defy the rigidly rooted traditional customs of marriage and family strictures. The characters of Desai, Kamala Das, Shobha De, Nayantara Sahgal and Anees Jung, portray women who want their individual worth realized and attempt to defy the suffering that conventional society offers them. Despite many socio-cultural, physical and psychological handicaps, the Indian woman has dared to venture in searching for her independent identity and is passing through a transitional phase where she is trying to fix her priorities and re-define her identity.

The various predicaments faced by Indian women towards achieving this selfhood have led feminist writers in necessitating a conscious attempt to evaluate the causes of hindrances. They have very seriously taken up this issue and made it the central subject of their writings and discussions. The post-Independence literature has witnessed women personas who have moved away from the traditional, enduring, self-sacrificing entities, towards a more vibrant and conflicting individual searching for an independent place in society. Indian woman "wanted to be whole"[7] and this pursuit of womanhood is well portrayed in the fictional characters of women writers. Though a lot has changed and the old archetype has been replaced with new prototype, yet at the grassroot level, Indian woman's "identity crisis" still persists. Her present state is so complex and precarious that it has assumed a totally different pattern in relation to the post-modernist approaches. Recalling Simone de Beauvoir's remark seems most appropriate to illustrate the present state of Indian woman: "The situation of woman is that she—a free and autonomous being like all creatures—nevertheless finds herself living in a world where man compel her to assume the status of the Other."[8]

Identity Crisis of the Indian Woman

Quest for identity by the Indian women writers had, till lately, not been a subject of great priority. Having analyzed the image of the Indian woman from the literature of the ancient to the present day, the future has to be drawn out rectifying the past mistakes. With the growth of feminism and feminist movement, women have become aware and conscious of their selfhood. This consciousness has led them to the search for an independent identity, which has become a fundamental concern and has gained much impetus. A whole group of women writers has emerged and taken up the issue as a major theme of their writings. Women have universally united to affirm their position and literature has become their familiar and influential medium of communication and expression. Indian English literature has become a canvas in depicting Indian woman's desire and urge for an unregimented selfhood and many women writers have employed it as a forceful medium to assert their views. Their outlook can be understood by studying the different shades of women characters presented in their works. Female protagonists in the fiction of Nayantara Sahgal, Meera Mahadevan, Shobha De, Ruth Prawer Jhabvala, Attia Hossain and Anita Desai will be discussed to comprehend their viewpoints of establishing an independent selfhood.

Sonali Ranade in Nayantara Sahgal's novel *Rich like Us* is depicted as a strong-willed, emotionally independent woman. Sonali grows up with a dream—to build a new convention and to prove her self-determining worth. Her survival instinct is so strong and instead of giving in, she gives up. Her resignation is not her acceptance of defeat; rather, it is her defiance against the oppressive forces, depicting her refusal to cringe before forces acting against her identity. It is Sonali's unique manner of asserting her individuality that is depicted in her behaviour and her decisions. She refuses to bow before the stranglehold of patriarchy and is a mistress of indomitable spirit.

A similar resolute persona is presented in the novel *Mistaken Identity*. The nameless but certainly not the faceless Ranee of Vijaygarh is a woman who dares to disseminate the concept of freedom and self-realization and differs from the praxis of the patriarchal society. The Ranee of Vijaygarh defies all moulds and definitions and distinguishes herself as a class apart, enforcing her independent principles. She prostrates before the deities to get a child, not to fulfill the need of hierarchy but to express herself through it. Her pining for the child is symbolic of her search for identity. Even when she marries comrade Yusuf, it is without any inhibitions. She walks her own proud way even when there is no comrade in her life. Ranee of Vijaygarh, though a nameless character, stands as a representative of womanhood, who marks the culmination of the onward march of Sahgal's new woman towards independence and freedom.

Shulamith, the central figure of Meera Mahadevan's novel *Shulamith*, depicts the experiences of a woman who experiences a "sense of dual fidelity" between her devotion to her husband and to her own way of life. The development of her selfhood and the assertion of her personality is brought out in her decision-making ability. She chooses her way of life and remains in India when her husband leaves for Israel. Though Mahadevan portrays Shulamith as ambivalent, makes Shulamith enforce social traditionalism and religious orthodoxy, a character to be highly respected. The writer sympathizes with both sides of the conflict but essentially has admiration for the strong-willed women who endure to achieve a selfhood.

Karuna in Shobha De's novel *Socialite Evenings* also is a vehement expression of individuality and assertion voiced overtly. Karuna, the young and ambitious girl from a middle-class family, yearns for high-class society life and realizes her ambition by entering the glamour world of modelling. She marries someone whom she feels will be a pedestal for her rise, but on realizing that her relationship is failure does not hesitate to break free. She breaks the conventional norms of silent suffering of a wife and starts a new relationship with Krish. On realizing the pitfalls of her second affair, she does not falter to live an independent life and overcomes all the sorrows and downfalls. She ultimately triumphs to be a successful and self-reliant woman without any male support. This shows her self-confidence and determination to achieve her independent stance and achieve her goal. The assertion of her selfhood is brilliantly depicted by De.

Sarla Devi in Ruth Jhabvala's *Get Ready for Battle* is another extrovert who gives priority to her identity and selfhood. Her need for self-expression drives her away from marital bonds. She takes up social service not as a means of escape but as a form of self-contentment and self-realization. Sarla Devi on understanding her incompatibility in marriage and the vast difference that lies between her husband, a materialist, and herself decides to take her own course in life. She separates from her husband and pursues her path of spiritual values and serving the oppressed and needy. She values her life and need of self-expression and is not ready to live as a shadow or as an appendage of her husband, sacrificing her principles.

Attia Hosain's protagonist Laila in *Sunlight on a Broken Column* is also a woman who faces the issue of repression and confronts the forces that suppress her personality. Laila is seen resolving and affirming her identity by rebellion and rejection and refuses to let her selfhood be destroyed. Her attachment to a man socially inferior to her is the confrontation between her own likes and principles of the family and mores of society. She emphasises her individuality when she makes her decision to stick to her likings, thereby proving that she has the confidence and courage to take her convictions to a logical conclusion. Her strength and determination to resist the dictates of the family and surrender to their likes proves that she identifies her independence and makes all efforts to assert her selfhood. Her demand and decision to choose her life partner, rejecting the false values of social and financial status, challenging the family rules and customs not just verbally but also in action, reveals her strength of character. Her dialogue, and behaviour makes it evident that Lila has an independent bent of mind which lead her to defying the old and worn-out conventions of society and affirm her selfhood.

Anita Desai's *In Custody* has the women characters who successfully defy traditional mores and assert their place in society. The Urdu poet's wife, who rages at her limitations and writes in her own defence, stands out as an outrageous persona. She radically redefines her experience by insisting on telling her story. Desai shocks us near the end of her novel when she presents Nur's young wife's point of view in a letter to Deven. She claims that Nur married because of her "gifts and abilities," and not because of sexual entrapment as had been assumed throughout the novel. Desai thus makes her protagonist's frustration understandable which gains her respect as a character by asserting her rights and abilities.

Thus a new trend of female characters can be witnessed in the modern fiction of women writers. Indian women even in dominant patriarchal society have started questioning the very basis of their roles, their place in the family and society, and above all their identity. Women began to overtly remonstrate against the age-old mores of the secondary status and relative identity given to them and raised their voice strongly in protest against it, through their literary works. The women writers explored the minds of educated, middle class woman and her search for a selfhood, the trials and tribulations that she faces, the physical and emotional upheavals that are her share in this journey of her quest for identity. The words of Shanta Krishnaswamy can be documented here to affirm the changes in the female protagonists of feminist fiction. According to her: "The passive feminine has ceased to exist. In her place we have the highly intelligent, sensitive woman who questions ceaselessly."[9]

Women Characters in Kamala Das's Fiction

Kamala Das's entry into the English literary scenario came like a thunderbolt breaking the long silence that was maintained about the Indian woman's life, her experiences, surroundings, family relationships, their trials and tribulations, love, sex etc. An outright feminist in her thought and behaviour, Das's fiction tried to fill the vacuum that was present in the Indian English literature. The Indian fictional works in English till the advent of Das were constrained to characters involved in love and romance, and were mostly dealt with in a superficial style portraying mythical typecasts. This type of writing was repressing and also misguiding of the factual life of the Indian woman on the whole.

Kamala Das broke the prevalent ideologies that surrounded woman and came up strongly with a new breed of literature and women characters. She blatantly refused to be bogged down by the women archetypes and created the "new Indian woman" in her literature, who went against the norms of society in quest of her individuation[10] and independence. As a writer who is concerned about women's predicament, she is a progeny of the matriarchal institution of Kerala society and also of a tradition where power itself is deified as goddess "Shakti," a female symbol. Das's fiction and female characters can be explained borrowing the words that Showalter employs in *A Literature of Their Own*:

> [Women writers] insisted upon the right to use vocabularies previously reserved for male writers and to describe formerly taboo areas of female experiences. For the first time anger and sexuality are accepted not only as attributes of realistic characters but also . . . as sources of female creative power.[11]

Das can incontrovertibly be labelled as an ardent follower of the principle that Mary Wollstonecraft preached in her feminist treatise *A Vindication of the Rights of Woman* published in 1792, that the intellect would always govern and sought

> to persuade women to endeavour to acquire strength, both of mind and body, and to convince them that the soft phrases, susceptibility of heart, delicacy of sentiment, and refinement of taste, are almost synonymous with epithets of weakness. It would be an endless task to trace the variety of meanness, cares, and sorrows, into which women are plunged by the prevailing opinion, that they were created rather to feel than reason, and that all the power they obtain, must be obtained by their charms and weakness.[12]

Reading through each of Kamala Das's short stories, it is quite evident that she tries to fuse the fragments of female feelings through an artistic visualization and is apprehensive about the independence and individuality of the Indian womanhood. Das also strongly advocates the fact that 'a society that fails to respect its women may have a great past but it can never have a great future.' Das strongly endorses the principle that Gandhiji had opined in his autobiography: "Womanhood is not restricted to the kitchen. Only when the woman is liberated from the slavery of the kitchen, that her true spirit may be discovered."[13]

Most of Kamala Das's women characters develop from the situations owing to their deep-rooted and poignant involvement with their past, love, marriage, family, home including generation gap. And it is from within the midst of these that woman has been searching for her place in the family and society, as an independent being. In a nutshell it can be stated that the quest for identity is the most overriding and prominent feature of woman characters that Das has tried to tackle in all her short fictional works.

The short stories of Kamala Das handle one or many of the singular issues concerning identity. The multiplicity of identity presented in stories of Das will help women analyze who they are, where they are headed and what obstacles must be crossed in the realization of their self and identity. A study of women characters in Das's short fictional works will help identify the various predicaments of their identity leading to the beginning of a positive introspection of the subject.

Motif of Identity in Das's Short Stories

The quest of identity can indisputably be seen as the most enduring and dominating motif in all the nineteen short stories that Kamala Das has published under the title *Padmavati, the Harlot and Other Stories.*[15] Each of these stories seeks to posit the independent subsistence of women and atrophy all attempts to preclude them from the centrestage of human existence. Das's approach to the attempts of attenuating women-power is holistic and focuses mainly on the question of identity crisis for women. Das, like Nayantara Sahgal, believes:

> Through the rewriting women do, new Sitas and Savitris will arise, stripped of false sanctity and crowned with the human virtue of courage. Then at last we will know why they did what they did, and how their lone, remote struggles can help our search for identity and emancipation.[14]

Kamala Das has tried to focus upon the place of woman in society and the vast number of physical and emotional problems relating to her existence and survival. She has sought to identify, define and discuss the various predicaments facing the Indian woman in her day-to-day living. The medium of short fiction has convincingly been employed by Das to express the Indian woman's search for her identity and in asserting herself both in the family and society. The analysis of her stories is a search in the manifestation of the various characters' quest for identity and also examines the autobiographical undertones present in them.

Das's most influential and thought-provoking stories are those dealing with the physically exploited women of society. "Padmavati, the Harlot" is a mind-boggling story of the woman who willingly becomes a harlot to sustain her family and their needs. Das has carefully selected the name and sketched her protagonist's character and brightened it by a rare mythical touch, which though inconceivable, is undoubtedly her own creation and masterpiece. A woman fallen and abhorred in the eyes of her family, friends and society is raised to the highest position of veneration by Das in the course of journey from the protagonist's house to the shrine and back. The writer does this in such a quick and convincing manner that the reader is made to acknowledge the characters' deed as justifiable and treat her with reverence and concern. Das portrays her as the chosen and beloved one of God whose purity of mind and soul is marked higher than those ostensibly virtuous people of society.

Padmavati, who wastes her life serving and slaving for her near and dear ones, is finally rejected when their need is over. She, in her course of life, was so occupied with the thoughts and well being of others that she forgot all about herself and her desires. The last bit that she gets in return from her family and society, for all the sacrifice and dedication she had rendered was to be thrown out as an outcast. It is at this point of time when left alone that she gets time to think about herself, her identity and her worth. The answer to her query and quest is received in the shrine of the Lord on the seven hills, a place she had been longing to visit since the past thirty-three years.

Das endorses the identity and respect for Padmavati by making the 'loafers' who mocked at her on the hillside 'winding passes' to the shrine with 'lewd smiles' and insulting remarks as: "You are not young, but you are charming enough for one evening or two. Your breasts still firm. Your haunches set our loin on fire. Won't you be kind enough to grant us your favours?" (24) finally bow down with respect when she returns from the Lord's shrine and seeing her murmur, "Mother, go in safety, give us your blessings and go your way." (25) Thus the reversal of status from that of a despised prostitute, to a worshipped mother is created within a single orbit of the story.

In this story Das has tried to break the typecast harlots and the revulsion that their very image brings to mind. By rendering Padmavati with a positive touch of character, Das has in a way succeeded in giving her an identity of her own. This story of Das also finds semblance in her poem, "Lines Addressed to a Devadasi" in which Das describes the life of a devadasi as follows:

> Ultimately there comes a time . . .
> It is then that your desires cease
> And a homesickness begins
> And you sit on the temple steps
> A silent devadasi, lovelorn
> And aware of her destiny.[16]

Das sympathizes with the prostitutes who are victims of society's scorn and are forced to live a secluded life, unable to assert their individuality. She defends Padmavati's character and gives her a sense of self-esteem by epitomizing God's acceptance of her tarnished body, which she had sold for thirty-three years in order to steer her family to the safe shores of a comfortable life. Padmavati who experiences the ecstasy of a bride in the union with the Lord in His shine, is a suggestion made in support for these recluse women by the writer. Das's proposition being that these helpless women should not be judged by their standards in society, instead an effort to understand their predicaments should be made.

The title also spells out a parody of goodness and greatness like 'Akbar, the Great' and 'God, the Almighty.' Padmavati, the harlot also ruled her kingdom, which was her family and did all that she could for their welfare and well-being, and had no regrets about anything. Her humility coupled with her love and devotion towards her family runs all along the story. In an interview, Kamala Das commented on the exploitation of women by society in the following words, "Every weakness is saleable. This is where men and society get the chance to exploit her."[17]

Das in this story brings forth the crude reality that for a man; a woman is only an object of sexual commodity that can be bought for, at a very cheap cost. Men make women sell her sentiments and weakness in exchange of her body, as in the case of Padmavati, whose love and concern for her family was exploited by men, which drives her to prostitution. Being personally aware of the ramification of sexual oppression, she abhors abusing of a woman's body, and vehemently revolts against it with a Promethean constancy. Das herself comments, "Being female and being fully human were mutually exclusive."[18]

In her stories she brings to light men who after having used a woman to satisfy their lust, ostracize and demean her identity and tag her off as a pariah. It is this kind of social attitude of society that suppresses a woman's development and growth into a complete individual marring her identity. Though the experience of the protagonist at the temple shrine is implausible at a gross level, the story of Padmavati, the harlot does succeed in achieving the writer's desired target and in drawing the reader's attention. Das has also been triumphant in making her protagonist assert her identity and command a certain degree of respect from the very society that has been responsible for her deplorable position by rendering Padmavati's sincerity towards her work as a *sadhana*.

A similar character is depicted in another short story of Das titled "The Princess of Avanti." Das introduces both satire and irony in the title itself to depict her animosity against the society that is totally malignant at the very core. The old practice of *Swayamvaram* is parodied with the insane woman waiting eagerly for a suitable bridegroom. The depiction of false identity of a mentally disturbed woman is what finds portrayal in this Das story. Her lack of a strong individual identity is what society exploits and misuses. Since she is an invalid having no social stronghold in society, men are free to behave in any manner and go away scot-free. Both Padmavati and the princess of Avanti stand as images of downtrodden women, questing for an identity and respectable place in society which results in their repression by men. Women are mere symbols of sex, whose body is looked upon as a toy for men to play with. The callous attitude with which the men who have raped and killed her converse shows how intimidating the question of women's identity has become in society.

> "Is she dead?" He asked his companions.
> "Perhaps," said the youngest. (18)

Das, both as a writer and as an individual, has always revolted against the physical humiliation and the degradation that women have to undergo. It is not just the individual identity of a woman, but also the collective gender identity of the female community that has been regarded as inferior. The attitude of men in not conceding women an independent entity has been continuing since genesis, beginning with Eve, who is believed to be made from "a supernumerary bone of Adam.' Aristotle declared that, "the female is a female by virtue of certain lack of qualities."[19] "Suppression as a legitimate form of self-control has long been recommended for women."[20] To prove her incompetence to protect her being and to keep her dependent and under his rule, men often resort to physical abuse of women. The instances of eve-teasing, rape, molestation and prostitution in Das's stories "The Princess of Avanti," "Padmavati, the Harlot" and "A Doll for the Child Prostitute" prove this.

Kamala Das is a writer who is extremely sensitive about the deep-rooted relation that lies between the female body and female identity. Her scale in judging society's attitude towards women is by the measure of respect and honour it renders to the woman's body. Man's response to the woman's body is chronicled by Das in all her works, and she makes man realize that it is through the female body that a man achieves completion. This feeling is recorded in the following lines of Das, "It was my desire that made him male, and beautiful."[21] She thus triumphs in establishing the fact that a woman's body is what makes her identity complete and complements a man's personality and by abusing the female body man in fact demeans his own worth and being. Das resents the male exploitation of female body and endorses Kate Millet's opinion that "puritanical conviction that sexuality is indeed dirty and faintly ridiculous."[22]

Two of her stories significantly handle the single woman concept, where the protagonist is shown capable to stand by herself defending her dignity and identity. She is shown neither dependent on men, nor is she susceptible to the womanly sentiments. She faces her situation with self-determination and self-realization. In "That Woman," Das brilliantly presents the much-slandered 'Other Woman' concept. This woman is not deterred by the identity of a mistress and happily adorns this illegal and vilified position because of her genuine love for the married man. The Indian woman is a product of a parochial society where women are so conditioned that it is not without a sense of guilt that they pursue their own independent stance. In the story Das's protagonist takes her individual decision of staying with a married man whom she loves, without any feeling of guilt and repentance. On his death, she is forced to leave the house she had shared with this man by his lawful wife and son. She has no hesitation to leave, which is well depicted in her words, "No . . . there is nothing of mine remaining here." (15) Her strength of will and her self-justification in her decision are well explained in the following lines by Das: "As she walked along the street in her crumbled cotton sari, I expected her to look back at least once but she did not. 'Ah, Stree.'" (15)

This woman in Das's story is bold enough to confront patriarchy's convention of man-woman relationship, and ascertain her own identity as an independent individual. One can note the feminist in Das coming to life in this character, who is strong-willed, emotionally independent woman refusing to bow before social norms. The story also brings to light the refusal of man to abide by the very same rules that he formulates for women like fidelity and commitment in marriage. A married man's extra-marital relationship is not considered with contempt or disgrace, when compared to that of a woman who gets involved in such affairs. Das emphasizes that going against the conventions and breaking the mores of society never tarnish man's identity but a woman's identity is always at stake, and she ends up being scorned by all.

As a writer, Das tries to drive home the point that woman should make an effort to assert her true self and free herself from the shackles created for her by family and society. It is only when women gain confidence in themselves and their individuality that men will realize their worth and learn to respect them. This is the theme that finds prominence in her next story "The Sea Lounge" where Das presents a woman who calmly walks out of her lover's life when she is rebuffed and rejected by him, without any emotional breakdown. Here the writer advocates that quest of identity may be a Herculean task for a woman who has been under the love and protection of a man, but once she learns to value her prestige and has strong will and determination not to be treated as a door-mat, she can definitely assert her identity. The convention of a single woman is well laid down in both these stories by Das, against the conformist society, which does not consent women to hold their own, and considers the very concept of female identity as preposterous. The character of the story stays unperturbed by her lover's refusal to marry her, astonishing him by her extraordinary serenity and poise. His anticipation of her begging him for love is reflected in the lines:

> Would she weep, would she once more proclaim her passionate love for him as she did in her last two letters and create now an unsavoury scene? . . . hoping that she would once again talk of her need for him, hoping that she would give him another chance. (19)

In portraying women characters, Das actually employs this strong feminine attitude to shatter the traditionally tailored Indian woman's reaction of begging and pleading, when jolted by her lover or husband. She is reckoned as a woman who disseminates the concept of freedom and self-respect and more importantly does so without the supporting crutches of men. The nameless woman in "The Sea Lounge" dares to differ in her approach and attitude in handling a broken affair. She is depicted as one who is not ready to compromise her pride and personality for a man who does not care to love her, leave alone marry her. Her unperturbed reply to him about her future plans shows her composure and will power of not being deterred even in the face of odds. She is in total control of herself and is able to make her own decisions without any remorse.

> She said, that is all right, I understand, please don't have a guilty conscience about me. . . . I will marry my old beau, she said, the one who has been crazy about me for years. Let us not worry about it now. Tell me about your new job. (21)

It is this self-reliance and self-affirmation of her identity that makes her elegant and wanted by the same man, who a short while ago had affronted her. Once again Das is victorious in presenting the reality, that when a woman appreciates her own worth and personage, she is valued and yearned for by men. The following lines express the same:

> With an ache in the pit of his stomach he realized that all the beauty of his life was going away with her. She was going away from him with no promise of a letter or a meeting. Everything between them was ended. In a panic he said, may I give you a lift, I can drop you wherever you want to go. (21)

Das seems to endorse Nayantara Sahgal's opinion, "It takes half of life to achieve personhood but there is no greater glory." (30)

The female identity in its vibrant shades, in the man-woman relationship, is deftly sketched in seven of Das's subsequent stories. Being a receptive feminist, Das's stories throw new light on the wide range of women characters. Her stories demonstrate profound apprehension about the perilous state of women in the parochial society. She seems to agree with David McReynolds observation, "nor can a person find his identity in the family-for that institution is breaking up."[23]

She does away with the Sita-Savitri-Sati typecast and rebuffs the Indian conventional role model wife. In her hands, the archetype Indian wife gets a revolutionary treatment and she is presented as one shattering all the chaste virtues of loyalty and purity. Kamala Das subscribes to the view of Betty Freidan who declared:

> For women as men, the need for self-fulfilment, autonomy, self-realization, independence, individuality, self-actualization is as important as the sexual need, with as serious consequences when it is thwarted.[24]

"The Youngman with the Pitted Face" is a deeply nostalgic story having overtures of Das's personal experience when she was hospitalized in a similar condition. Though it speaks about a mutual marital infidelity of a young handsome married man and a middle-aged married woman in ill health, the essentially embedded theme is that of an identity crisis, which the sick woman is confronting. Das has enlivened a part of her own experience in this story, which finds mention in the various accounts of ill health, in her autobiography. The need and desire to be loved and cared, makes her accept the love from an unfamiliar man. Her quest for love and its fulfilment gives her the strength to fight and survive even the gravest health problem. It is definitely the strength of her character and her personal desire that dares her to venture into a love relation with a married man younger to her, overlooking the established social and moral norms laid down for a wife. The realization of her wishes and aspirations and giving it importance and priority over others, is in itself, a step towards self-assertion. She does not bother to reflect about how her decision will be countered by her family and society and is all set to live her life on her own terms. Even in the face of an impending death looming large, she dares to live, think and act according to her own preferences and likes. She learns to assert herself through her decisions in accepting the love of an anonymous man not knowing how and where this relation will take her. She is not ready to thwart her love for this unfamiliar man, whatever its consequences might be, showing a grit that is generally objectionable to society and deemed offensive on the part of a married Indian woman.

The woman character in this story shows a breaking away from the restrictive and repressive influences of social norms as well as from the shaping influences of family and society to emerge as an individual true to her being. On realizing the consolation this young married man's love is giving her, during the precarious stage of her physical suffering, she gathers courage to accept and respond to it without a second thought. It is at this point of distress that she firmly stands her ground and decides to live her life. She has neither any guilt nor remorse even when this lover fails to turn up and has enough strength of mind to accept the same. Her emerging from a timid to a self-confident and assertive individual, bold enough to make her own decisions and face its consequences is well portrayed in the following lines:

> It was only a month old, . . . He was the youngest . . . man she had ever loved, and the situation frightened her. She said tomorrow he will be here . . . and tomorrow he will again take my hands in his and everything will be beautiful. . . . In the morning, her nurse dressed her up like a bride, knowing how deeply in love she was. (31-35)

The story titled "December" is centred on a woman writer who has recently recovered from 'a long illness.' She continues with her extra-marital affair, which she had promised God to give up, if she recovered fully. But after recovery, she is unable to keep her word and the reason for it is made overt in the following lines: "she thought happiness is so simple, just walk into his room and lie down and I am happy, but I am a happiness-addict, that is my problem." (37) She does not hesitate to break her promise and has no sense of remorse doing the same. "The promise had worked out but she was going to break her words and with no great qualms either." (36) Though a little depressed at losing her talent in writing which she had so passionately liked to do, she has no doubts about her priorities in life. Her ability to list her choices and give up the ones which come in the way of her happiness, is acted upon with confidence and least repentance:

> while tears rose in her eyes, . . . he asked, you don't have any doubts, do you and, she kissed his eyes . . . whispering no, no, not anymore, but though I have become soft and sentimental, I shall never be able to write again, I am finished. (37)

Like "The Youngman with the Pitted Face," "December" is also a sentimental piece but with the execution of a bold resolution of a woman, who gives greater value to the fulfilment of love and has the nerve to break even her promise given to God. Her decision not to forfeit her love for her profession and family confirms the rendering of her strong sense of individualism and free will.

Kamala Das's next story with the rebel attitude of woman is "A Little Kitten." The story depicts the change in identity of an innocent and coy wife on apprehending her husband's indifferent attitude shortly after their honeymoon. The "mysterious silence" (38) that the husband observes when probed about his relation with Miss Nadkar makes the wife hysterical. She is a typical Indian wife whom her husband considered "a sweet and innocent creature." (38) After getting to know her husband's extra-marital relation, she had withdrawn into her own cocoon. This initial gloominess and nervousness is soon overcome and before long her outlook is altered. She is quick to decide about her life and decides not to waste it and sacrifice her happiness for the sake of a man who is not bothered about her. Das very aggressively reacts to the attitude of sexual freedom that men take for granted. She expresses her intense desire for a sexual revolution. Her intention in all her stories has been to shake the Indian woman from her inert, meek, diffident attitude into awakening.

At the close of the story, one fine day when the husband arrives home he is stunned to see his wife once again in full bloom, with a scratch mark above her breast. The husband thinks that the mark on his wife's neck is caused by a kitten, but the truth being that she has retaliated to his infidelity by committing adultery; in other words, she has played the same game that her husband had been practising. Her betrayal is seen as a fidelity to self, and her quest for perfect love. It is her search for her self and her self-assertion that finally made her take revenge for her husband's faithlessness. Her strength to endure and solve her own family problems is drawn in her decision not to go to her parents' place alone for a change as suggested by her husband. Das also implies that being autonomous in one's own judgments and decisions is the only way to develop ones identity.

"Darjeeling" is a story where the husband's financial reservations and personal matters are weighed higher that his wife's illness. Sitting in the ambulance with his wife who is serious, his thoughts remain concerned neither about her health, nor her recovery; instead he is disturbed thinking about his financial matters.

> The husband sat on the narrow seat opposite, clutching the doctor's letter and brooding over his finances. . . . If she were to die today . . . he would not be able to give her anything better than the electric crematorium. . . . If she were to pull through, the hospital would fleece him all right. (42)

Das through this story questions the position of a wife in a man's life. Das tries to present the insignificance of a woman's life and problems when compared to the man's predicaments. As depicted in the story, it is not the wife who is more important to him but his finance. The pettiness with which he talks to the doctor about his wife, exhibits how unimportantly she is treated:

> The honorary called him aside and whispered, . . . It was a heart attack. . . . It is rare in women of her age. . . . I wouldn't have believed it, did she suffer any mental strain, any secret tension? . . . I don't think so, said the husband, she is not the worrying type, I do all the worrying at home. (43)

The husband's ignorance about his wife's state of mind shows that she had no credible place in his life and her presence and identity is of no particular importance. The husband's indifferent and uncaring attitude once again is figured when he sits thinking about his letter-drafting ability and the appraisal his boss had showered him with, while even the toddler is anxious about his mother. A woman's identity is well put to query here and through it Das champions the quest for self-identity to her sisterhood. Das asks women not to behave like self-sacrificing goats and inspires them to develop self-awareness and self-worth and strongly assert their individuality.

In the story "The Sign of the Lion," Das portrays a middle class woman's quest for her self. It is her desire to be loved by someone higher and wealthier than her in society that attracts her to this man about whom everyone cautions her. "Some people desire to climb a mountain. Some people wish to go to the moon. All I ever wanted was to possess someone superior." (46) It is her wish and interest that makes her shun society's outlook about this man who is a known womanizer, but she does not care as she finds in his company freedom of self-expression and financial security, which her social background lacks: "He is a rich man. I am moderately poor. The rich, I think, are supermen; they are on their way to becoming Gods." (46) She is not concerned about the future, instead she wishes to live in the present and its happiness and as long as he needs her love. "He is afraid of the dark. Once, when I switched off the light, he clung to me. . . . What are you afraid of, my baby-boy, I asked him. Do not be afraid. I am with you." (46)

She is a woman whom Das records as exhibiting exemplary strength to live her life as she wills, and challenge its consequences. "I am never secure. That goes without saying. If my feet were secured on the ground, my mind would fall asleep. But this way with my feet off the ground, my mind leaps, it flies." (46)

She is one whose visions of self-hood are not clouded by conventions. She knows not only what she wants but also how to achieve it. Understanding the uncertainty of his behaviour and no commitment of his love, she takes all measures to keep hold of him by taking the risk of bearing his child.

> They say that he will take me to Lonavala and with tenderness kill me.
>
> I tell him of the child to come. He will be a little lion, I tell him. A beautiful lion-cub. (48)

This unrelenting soul wants to produce a child not because she considers it essential for hierarchy, but because she wants to secure her needs and assert her presence and personality through it. Her pining for a child is symbolic of her affirmation of selfhood.

"Sanatan Choudhuri's Wife" is a story dealing with the theme of mistaken identity. It has, at the same time, an undercurrent showing the defencelessness of an Indian wife's identity when doubted by her husband. Her individuality is an element of constant suspicion and distrust to the husband as can be witnessed in this story. Even after six years of committed married life, Gopi Menon suspects his wife. She is subjected to doubts and disbelief even at the slightest provocation. The utterance of a male name in her dream makes the husband Gopi Menon apprehensive about his wife. The very fact that a wife who has lived with him for six years is suspected, is an insult to the woman. Das has emphatically voiced her negation of the husband's act of inspecting the wife's wardrobe and enquiring about the source of finance she got in purchasing her saris. Das feels that it is an abuse to womanhood to be followed around and questioned with the intention of checking and confirming to the man's satisfaction her chastity and fidelity. "When he was standing on the platform waiting for the fast train to Bandra, he suddenly decided to put her to a test, to clear his own mind of suspicions." (50) The old Hindu myth of Lord Rama asking Sita to undergo the fire test to confirm her chastity is brought to the reader's mind. Though times have changed, the mentality and outlook of man still remains the same. Das in these stories also highlights the approach of men and their commitment to the bonds of marriage. Das echoes Simone de Beauvoir's observation about the same:

> Man marries today to obtain an indenture anchorage in immanence, but not to be himself confined therein; he wants to have hearth and home while being free to escape therefrom; he settles down but often remains a vagabond at heart; he is not contemptuous of domestic felicity, but he does not make of it an end in itself, repetition bores him; he seeks novelty.[25]

This male attitude of double standards where the wife is expected to be chaste and maintain fidelity and the man having his own free will is vehemently disputed by Das in a number of her stories like "The Kitten" and "The Other Woman." It is this reluctance to accept woman as his equal and treat her with respect, that Indian women have been denied an identity and stature of their ability. There is the general attitude of man to think that women can't do anything right because they are 'only' women and man is always susceptible to physical and material attractions. It is this attitude of men that needs change. The traditional outlook assigned to woman is more of patriarchy's convenience for having the reigns of power and authority in their hands. In short it is a matter of social decision and convenience. Das thus underlines the fact that women need to stand on their own and assert themselves in their position not only as a wife, mother and sister but also as an individual and it is only then that she can prove her worth to society

Das casts her characters in the traditional mould in the beginning and slowly develops them as strong individuals internally and externally. A point of reference in these stories of Das is that though it is about the woman's quest of identity, it does not confirm to the feminist viewpoint or create a world without men. Though the women find contentment in making their independent decisions based on their personal happiness and desire, men do play a significant role in helping them emerge as individuals in their own right.

The unveiling of a woman in the role of a wife, her duties and responsibilities, her sentiments, her worries and apprehensions find mention in "Walls" and "Grandfather." But the primary aspect of women's identity that Das deals with in both these stories is that of the new relative identity molded through social status that a woman gets when she is married. The identity of an Indian wife is inevitably fashioned on the basis of her relation with her husband. It is in this quest for a secure and comfortable life that woman finds gratification in living as a happy and ideal wife. Though a lot of compromise goes into making this relative identity work out well, as mentioned in Das's poem *The Descendants*:

> But,
> I must pose,
> I must pretend,
> I must act the role
> of a happy woman
> happy wife.[26]

It is also shown to render a sense of fulfilment and delight. These women are not static beings; instead they have grown and changed according to the surrounding, which is an important part of one's identity. To accept changes and change with it, by developing one's personality is in the true sense an assertion of one's identity. Therefore by adorning the identity of a wife, women need not restrict their self-growth, nor do they need to lose their individuality, instead they can by understanding their priorities in life, find peace and happiness.

In the story titled "Walls," Das portrays a caring wife who changed herself from a village girl to a modern woman, in order to blend with her new married life and the new identity that she has got. It is undoubtedly her wish for the modern life style and the happiness of her loved ones that she has transformed herself. She has changed herself so much that even her husband is surprised. He reminisces about the days before marriage when she "had revealed her wishes to him, . . . had he not forgotten those days, the brief season when the two of them dared to bare their ambitions, their desires?" (103)

She has positively employed the new surroundings to develop her personality and changed drastically, adopting to the new life, which has astonished him beyond doubt:

> The middle-aged woman sporting pastel silks and diamond jewellery was his wife, this city slick woman who spoke in several lan-

> guages. . . . Had she not changed within as imperceptibly as she had changed in her appearance over the years? Was she the Madhavi he had carried away from her village-home, her shyness as glittering as her wedding silks? (103)

Self-development leads to personal growth, which assists in the better understanding and assertion of one's rights and authority. The character of Madhavi the village girl depicts her capacity of being able to control and efficiently manage her home and all its members, due to her self-maturity. She has neither regret nor dissatisfaction in her life as compared to her husband who in spite of achieving all that he had aimed for is totally frustrated and isolated. The story also highlights the fact that muscular power and dominance is not the pre-requisite of being loved and respected by people. Though it is the men who rule, it is always the woman whose support and companionship makes a man complete and the family content. This is well etched out in the final conversation of the story:

> Am I preparing a balance sheet of my spent years, he asked himself. . . . That night, before falling asleep, he said, "Madhavi, I want to resign from my job." She did not seem upset.
>
> "Why?"
>
> "I want to return to my village home. After all we two are no longer young."
>
> She smiled. A gust of wind clamped the windows shut. Outside a heavy downpour was in the offing. (106)

These lines clearly state that Madhavi has been successful in making a niche for herself in the family and society and the husband finally opening his mind to her is a proof of his acceptance of her as an independent and level-headed individual whose presence he needs in his life. Her identity has thus been well emphasized even though she makes an obedient and caring wife.

In the story "Grandfather," though old age is the issue discussed, the moot point once again is that Das has tried to emphasize the decision-making ability of a woman caught between the meshes of her own family and her old father's desire. For her, both her husband and father are equally important and she makes her choice after careful assessing the situation. Her decision not to take her old father with her to a far-off city is made by her independently after analyzing the practical aspects of the situation. Though a little upset by her father's persistent demand to take him with her to Bombay, her initial hesitation to decide on the issue is overcome. Thankam finally weighs the matter not as a sentimental person but as a mature adult, practical, sensible and composed in her thoughts. Realizing that the old father is being temperamental and that she will be unable to attend to his needs and also looking into her constraints knowing very well that he will not be able to adjust to the life and atmosphere of a new place like Bombay, she makes the final resolution to console him with the promise of visiting him after six months. Thus, the protagonist proves herself to be an assertive and independent individual capable of managing her problems without anybody's assistance.

Maternal sentiments are the focus in "Moongphali," "The Tattered Blanket," and "Leukaemia." The female identity identified in motherhood assumes great significance and given the basic difference between male and female psychology, women possess what Sara Ruddik calls the "maternal thinking"[27] which is life-sustaining. This is evident in the above-mentioned stories of Kamala Das. In "Moongphali," Das has incorporated many topics varying from political issues to the basic human sentiments which are unaffected by religion, caste or creed. In spite of diverse issues handled by Das in this story, the important theme presented is that of woman's need for self-realization. Here Das portrays Jasmit's mother who is extremely sensitive about her daughter and granddaughter. Having lived and experienced the hardships of life, she tries to be cautious not to let her daughter have a similar fate in life. She is an assertive old lady who refuses to be cheated even by the auto driver. Her firm stand about the auto fare and her forcefulness is expressed in her conversation with the auto driver, "I shall not give you one paisa more than what I had promised you at the railway station." (7) Her strength of mind and her identity as a Sikh, which she so much emphasizes preventing her from behaving like a coward even at the sight of mob fury. Her strength, to face the situation, is noticed in her dialogue with her son-in-law:

> Go and fight, you eunuch, cried the old woman, pushing her son-in-law out of the yard. Don't behave like a coward. You are a sardar and never for a moment should you forget it. (13)

Das has also tried to present the shady elements like the auto driver, prevalent in society about whom women should be watchful. The old woman is shown as extremely sensitive about her daughter who she feels is not astute enough. The writer, through the character of the old mother, shows that the world is basically an unsafe place for a woman and so she should be shrewd and vigilant. A woman in quest of identity should always keep herself updated with the happenings of her surroundings and be well-equipped to guard herself. Das vehemently opposes the conventional attitude of women in keeping off from the activities taking place in the society and the world around her. Says Jasmit:

> I don't know these things, Mother, said the young woman, I am not a woman who bothers about politics. I look after my child and feed my husband. These are my duties. Let the Prime Minister look after the country. (9)

She strongly recommends women's participation in the activities of the society, which in turn will lead to self-understanding and self-confidence and give her power to assert and think as an independent human being.

"Leukaemia" is another touching story of a woman who in order to train and build her child's personality sends her off to a boarding school. In her effort and ambition to groom her daughter into a well mannered and sophisticated lady, she makes the resolution but is shattered on knowing about the child's illness. The mother's sentiments and sorrow at losing her daughter are so profound that she gives up all her strictness. The story makes clear that the mother actually suppresses her motherly sentiments for the betterment of the child when deciding to send the child to the boarding school and at the child's departure after vacation, she consoles herself by keeping away from the sight of the departing child. "At the beginning of each New Year, he took a screaming child [. . .] the mother hid herself in the bedroom giving as an excuse her weak heart." (65) A mother's wish to educate and build her daughter into a self-reliant refined and independent individual with the best of traits is in the mother's wish.

The central idea that can be traced in this story is the affirmation of a woman's identity as a mother who sacrifices her own sentiments and considers it her responsibility to groom her child into an individual with a positive and respectable personality. It is the cruelty of fate and not her decision of sending the child to the boarding school that had resulted in the child's disease. Here the words of Robin Morgan can be quoted about women's quest in motherhood as "crucial to the continuation of sentient life on this planet."[28]

The story "The Tattered Blanket," has another very skilfully-handled character, with a word of caution for women dependent on their sons, brothers etc. The story shows the difficulties encountered by the widowed woman and her eighty-five year old mother. Though womanly sentiments dominate the story from the start to the end, it simultaneously portrays through the son the male attitude towards woman. The son, who is an educated and financially well-placed man in society, keeps away from his mother and sister who are dependent on him. Instead of being of help and support to them, he comes over to visit them after five years to get his share of property so that he can secure his own future. The self-centred male attitude is well drawn by Das who has always advocated the need for woman's financial independence. Das has very cautiously tried to make women aware that she should learn to be self-sufficient and independent in her requirements, and try not to depend on anyone, husband, son or brother. She has very clearly depicted the ebbing away of human sentiments and the advent of a materialistic world where money and not human bonds dominate.

Women as mothers, sisters and wives struggle all through their life like unpaid servants to fulfill and make man's life happy and comfortable. But the moment she becomes old or unfit to tend to men's needs, they become liabilities and are shunned by their dear ones for whom she had slogged and struggled all through her life. It is only during such unforeseen moments of anguish, like the one mentioned by Das in this story does a woman start thinking about herself and her identity:

> Why have you come, she asked him. It is not merely to see *Amma*, is it?
>
> My expenses have increased, the man said, now I have four children. . . . I have to maintain my status and live decently. I want to sell my share of property. . . . I came to discuss this matter with you. (64)

The mother's selfless sacrifices are never remembered nor acknowledged, and man conveniently overlooks her needs when she grows old and dependent. It is not the old mother's requirement of a blanket but the share of property that he wants which the son considers more important. Das thus cautions women that they should learn to stand for themselves and be capable enough to be self-supportive and self-sufficient. It is dependence on men that tarnishes a woman's identity. Patricia Waugh has rightly mentioned in her book:

> Awareness of the arrest of feminine development brought about by an economic system, a family structure which produced in women dependency, insecurity, lack of autonomy and an incomplete sense of who they are.[29]

In the story "Equity Shares" there is the overriding emotion of an aged yet iron-willed and dignified woman who is passionately attached to her departed husband and anxious about her mentally challenged child. Her identity and dignity are well guarded by her even under the utmost financial crisis. Her decision not to part with her shares even for a handsome amount of money portrays the woman in her, confident and clear about her outlook in life. Even under the state of financial and mental catastrophe, she dares to stand by her decisions and face life challengingly. Her strength of mind not to sacrifice her prestige and self-esteem is a distinct mark of her selfhood. She is an example presented by Das for those women who have to live their life alone without the support of anyone. Defending one's individuality even under the most challenging situations is the moot point stressed by Das. In a society, which considers women as weak humans, unable to stand unaided without a strong protective male hand, this story of Das presents a different picture of womanhood. Here her protagonist is portrayed as hoisting the flag of gender-equality and seeking *carte blanche* for their race.

The identity attained in pristine motherhood is the theme in the next two stories of Das titled "The Coroner" and "Iqbal." The gift of motherhood is considered divine and it lends woman with a strength that is amazing. Woman's confidence in her self-entity is at its peak during this stage and she is seen to be sensitive and caring about even those who have done her nothing good. In the story "The Coroner," the pregnant lady is very happy in her new-found identity of motherhood and is particularly affectionate and sensitive to the distressed and lonely man who has lost his son. It is this motherly identity and response, which makes her so distressed on hearing about the coroner's son's untimely demise. She is immediately able to identify herself with the sentiments of the dead boy's mother and is abrupt in enquiring, "How will your poor wife ever get over this." (55) A woman's life is a continuous search for selfhood from a girl to that of a lover, a wife, mother etc. and each of these identities renders her more growth and assertive powers. A woman's quest for identity in motherhood, and the associated anxieties and apprehensions is what give vent to her feelings on listening to the old man's tragedy and the tears that swell up in her eyes is a result of it. Devindra Kohli in his book Kamala Das comments about motherhood in the following words, "The woman's pregnancy is a token of her individuality."[30]

Similar sensitivity is also witnessed in the story "Iqbal." Das has very brilliantly portrayed the expecting mother's change in attitude and the self-confidence with which she tackles her family problems. Her self-confidence and enthusiasm is drawn from her realization of motherhood making her very secure and assured about her position and identity in life.

Das asserts the fact that a woman is raised to a higher level of dignity and status, once she is blessed with maternity and this enhances her dignity and self-worth, which is witnessed in the change in her husband's attitude on seeing as her belly grows. The protagonist's independence and individuality is also seen to develop, with her initial anxiety on knowing about her husband's homosexual relation being completely overcome once it is confirmed that she is pregnant. She is seen as a more self-reliant person, and affirms her identity overtly to Iqbal when she visits him at the hospital where he is admitted after attempting suicide. Knowing that her motherhood was the cause that led Iqbal to commit suicide, she ridicules him, making him recognize his folly and at the same time assert her position. Her final words to him are:

> I know why you did it. . . . You are jealous of me, . . . You are jealous because it is not possible for you to become pregnant. . . .
>
> Get out of here you devil, hissed Iqbal, and instead of growing angry she only felt her heart growing lighter, and laughter bubbling up inside her throat. (60)

The path undertaken by the Indian woman in her quest for identity and its final assertion is a journey treaded in three stages. Beginning with a life lived in accordance with the conventional role enforced by family and society, to the dawn of self-acknowledgment of the dissatisfaction in adhering to these set norms, and finally her flouting out of this artificial and forced representation of her identity. In short, the journey of women characters in quest of identity is worked out within the framework of conflict, resolution and eventually in self-realization. The clash that all the protagonists in the stories confront is between living their lives as they wish to live and living it as their family and society wants them to. Their ultimate resolution of asserting and living their life according to their own will is portrayed as those, which end their submission to the societal norms and the heralding of their expression of individuality. The final pronouncement of these women indicates the confidence in attempting to rebuild their life prevailing over the distress and ruins of an unhappy love relation, or married life. The message conveyed by Das is that personal happiness and growth of woman must not be subordinated to the wishes of others. It expresses a belief in the possibility of 'self-culture' in the continuous growth of the soul.[31]

Kamala Das pleads that woman should have the freedom to be her own master and make decisions. Kamala Das craves for a more open atmosphere for women to live and draws the readers' attention to what Jill Johnston had said, "passivity is the dragon that every woman has to murder,"[32] and this alone will help her rise above the male domination. Moreover, women can identify, explore, and utilize their creative potential. The creative activity will help them actualize their real selves and will help them establish themselves as singular, sovereign subjects.

Woman's Assertion of Identity

The short stories of Das as a generic mode deployed for ascertaining woman's quest for identity, has been extremely successful and rewarding. According to Frank O'Connor, short stories are the cry of the lonely voice and depict lonely people on the fringes of society.[33] After analyzing at length each of her short stories, it can be stated that Das has tried to scrutinize the problems and predicaments of women on the issues of identity from all possible angles and in all possible roles. The writer's personal life experiences and her identity crisis, which she faced and fought all alone has been a motivating element in all her women characters' quest for self-realization. Jameela Begum has commented as follows about her short stories:

> The female identity for Kamala Das, thus, is an intricate mosaic that constantly throws up new lights and shades. Her women are strong and weak, whores and mothers, lovers and wives. The themes of her short stories capture women's identity in various situations and moods. . . . Diverse themes such as these give the short stories a richness that proclaims that there is not just "a truth" about woman's identity but many truths that coalesce and proclaim her multifaceted nature . . . so that at the end of a reading of such a collection, one is left with a dynamic and complex vision of woman.[34]

In order to have an identity of her own, the Indian woman needs to be liberated from the restrictions of age-old traditions and customs giving her a fair amount of space and freedom to think and decide for herself. Borrowing the words of Simone de Beauvoir:

> When the struggle to find one's own place in this world is too arduous, there can be no question of getting away from it. Now, one must first emerge from it into sovereign solitude if one wants to try to regain a grasp upon it: what woman needs first of all is to undertake, in anguish and pride, her apprenticeship in abandonment and transcendence: that is, in liberty. (56)

One of the main reasons why Indian woman has not been able to assert her identity can well be associated to what Simone de Beauvoir remarks in her book *The Second Sex*:

> Women do not contest the human situation, because they have hardly begun to assume it. This explains why their works for the most part lack metaphysical resonances and anger; they do not take the world incidentally, they do not ask questions, they do not expose its contradiction: they take it as it is too seriously. (56)

Another important factor that Das's fiction reveals is that a woman's identity cannot be affirmed without the understanding and expression of her sex. Her body like her mind needs freedom of expression and should be respected. Excluding the female body from their writings will hamper the self-expression and self-assertion capacity of a woman. So for a sincere quest for identity and a forceful assertion of the same, Kamala Das strongly campaigns the use of body language in her writings. Keeping aloof from this has caused the Indian women lag so far behind in their search for their being. She has accepted and absorbed diverse experiences and made use of physical exploitation of women to project the hardships women face in this journey for their search for identity. To quote Helene Cixous:

> Woman must write herself: must write about women and bring women to writing, from which they have been driven away as violently as from their bodies—for the same reasons, by the same law, with the same fatal goals. Woman must put herself into this text—as into the world and into history—by her own movement.[35]

Kamala Das feels strongly about female exploitation and male sarcasm towards the issue of women's identity-crisis. She demands social justice for women, her focus being on women's autonomy. Each of Das's stories has a depth of meaning, and the women characters portrayed in each of them have a great role to play in guiding and shaping Indian womanhood. They play a vital role in developing women's consciousness to make an endeavour and resolve to seek their identity, to discover and assert themselves, discarding submissiveness and developing conviction in their powers and potential, refuse deprivation, subordination, marginalization and victimization to "affirm" and "struggle to transform the circumstances which try to transform her."[36]

Das with an unassailable position among the prominent English poets proves to her English readers that her prose works are nothing less in comparison. One can agree with Rashmi Talwar who writes:

> It may be desirable for women writers in the future to portray a woman who does not adhere to or follow any model but is herself and is initiated into a search to discover her deeper identity.[37]

What can be contended about the 'identity-crisis' that Indian women face is that patriarchy's allegiance to traditions and conventions, myths and beliefs, culture and heritage are still the stumbling blocks in the path of emancipation. The need lies in coming to terms with living identity, as opposed to the fossilized ones and women need to contemplate on what Carlos Christ advocates in his book:

> Women's . . . quest includes moments of solitary contemplation, but it is strengthened by being shared. It involves asking basic questions: Who am I? Why am I here? What is my place in the universe? In answering these questions, a woman must listen to her own voice and come to terms with her own experience. Because she can no longer accept conventional answers to her question, she opens herself to the radically new—possibly to the revelation of powers or forces of being larger than herself and her position in the world.[38]

Hence the challenge lies in realizing the need to strike a balance with the changing time and also the similarities and differences among the sex and their gender relations. The necessity is in accepting the differences, but not demonizing it, realizing the fact that the two sexes are similar but not homogeneous. Another fact that needs to be comprehended is that tradition and customs can be valued but, if they do not adapt, they become instruments of oppression. In the words of Ziauddin Sardar:

> Identity has historic anchors but it is not fixed to a limited, unchanging set of traditional signs and historic symbols. Identity is not what we buy, or what we choose, or what we impose on others; rather, it is something from which we learn how to live, discover what is worth buying, and appreciate what it is to be different. The challenge is to change and yet remain the same.

Kamala Das has thus in her short stories created women protagonists who have refused to be mere puppets and deconstructed the dependent characters by developing in them assertive and independent behaviour. She has thus broken the "dependency syndrome"[39] of Indian women in her fiction and made them develop an individuality of their own. Indian women's quest for identity has been excellently depicted in all the nineteen short stories of Das in the collection titled *Padmavati, The Harlot and Other Stories*.

Conclusion

It can well be concluded that Das who is an original and innovative writer, has in her stories concentrated on the vast majority of middle class women of the Indian society. Knowing and understanding the dilemmas that these women have to continuously contend in life, Das has through her characters made obvious the change in attitude that has started taking place in society. The change in the woman's approach from the all-enduring nature to that of a more assertive attitude is a result of the change in social conditions and growing self-awareness of her rights as a human being. It no longer seems possible and reasonable to the educated women to accept a secondary position both in her family and society. Yet it cannot be denied that both the inner and outer world in which a woman lives and constantly interacts, still remains under the male ascendancy. Though efforts are being made to achieve a respectable position for woman, her place in society has yet to undergo any drastic changes. It is here that the authenticity of the writer Kamala Das and her avocations for equality of gender re-emerges and affirms its present-day needs.

The well-judged and sharp observation of Simone de Beauvoir needs to be recalled to make a comment of the present state of women in society and need for self-identity and self-assertion. Beauvoir observes:

> Woman herself recognizes that the world is masculine on the whole; those who fashioned it, ruled it, and still dominate it today are men. As for her, she does not consider herself responsible for it; it is understood that she is inferior and dependent; she has not learned the lessons of violence, she has never stood forth as subject before the other members of the group. Shut up in her flesh, her home, she sees herself as passive before these gods with human faces who set goals and establishes values. In this sense there is truth in the saying that makes her the "eternal child." . . . The lot of women is a respectful obedience. She has no grasp, even in thought, on the reality around her. It is opaque to her eyes. (609)

This attitude still persists and a lot of efforts still remain to be done to achieve equality of status and make women realize that they are masters of their own destiny.

NOTES

1. Qtd Ziauddin Sardar, "The A-Z of Postmodern Life," *New Statesman*, 25 Feb. 2002.
2. *Collier's Dictionary* (New York: Macmillan, 1990) 410.
3. *Collier's Dictionary*, 213.
4. John Stuart Mill, *The Subjection of Women* (London: Longman, Green, 1869) 141.
5. Veena Noble Dass, ed., *Feminism and Literature* (New Delhi: Prestige, 1995) 11.
6. Erik H. Erickson, *International Encyclopedia of Social Sciences*, ed. David L. Sills, Vol. 7 (London: The Macmillan and the Free Press, 1968) 61.
7. Margaret Atwood, *Surfacing* (New York: Simone and Schuster, 1972) 76.
8. Qtd. Sushila Singh, *Feminism and Recent Fiction in English* (New Delhi: Prestige, 1991) 22.

9. Shanta Krishnaswamy, *The Woman in Indian Fiction in English* (New Delhi: Ashish, 1984) 238-39.
10. The term individuation is defined as the need for autonomy and self-identity and this is central to Johanna Kirkpatrick's thesis in her paper, "Women in Indian English Literature: The Question of Individuation." *Journal of South Asian Literature*, XII, 3 and 4 (Spring 1977) 121-29.
11. Elaine Showalter, *A Literature of Their Own: British Women Novelists* (London: Virago, 1977) 34.
12. Mary Wollstonecraft, *A Vindication of the Rights of Women* (www.bartleby.com).
13. Mahatma Gandhi, *The Story of My Experiments with Truth*, trans. Mahadev Desai (Boston: Beacon Press, 1993).
14. Nayantara Sahgal, *Point of View* (New Delhi: Prestige, 1997) 33.
15. Kamala Das, *Padmavati, the Harlot and Other Stories* (New Delhi: Sterling, 1994), 24.
16. Lines Addressed to a Devadasi, *An Anthology of Indo-English Poetry*, ed. Gauri Deshpande (Delhi: Hind Pocket Books, n.d.) 30.
17. Interview with Smita Padmanabhan.
18. Qtd. Iqbal Kaur, ed., "Sexual Politics and Kamala Das," *Perspective of Kamala Das's Prose* (New Delhi: Intellectual, 1995) 145.
19. H.M. Parshley, Translator's Preface, Simone De Beauvoir, *The Second Sex* (Penguin, 1972) 22.
20. Patricia Meyer Spacks, *The Female Imagination* (London: Allen and Unwin, 1976) 93.
21. Kamala Das, *Summer in Calcutta* (New Delhi: Everest Press, 1965) 18.
22. Kate Millet, *Sexual Politics* (London: ABACUS, 1972) 5-6.
23. David McReynolds, "Hipsters Unleashed," *The Beats*, ed. Seymour Krim (Greenwich: Faucett, 1960) 203.
24. Betty Freidan, *The Feminine Mystique* (Harmondsworth: Penguin, 1971) 9.
25. Simone de Beauvoir, *The Second Sex*, 475.
26. Kamala Das, "The Suicide" *The Descendants* (Calcutta: Writers' Workshop, 1967) 2.
27. Sara Ruddik, "Maternal Thinking," *Feminist Studies* 6:2 (Summer 1980) 348.

28. Robin Morgan, *The Anatomy of Freedom* (New York: Doubleday, 1982) 282-84.
29. Patricia Waugh, *Feminine Fictions: Revisiting the Postmodern* (London: Routledge, 1989) 85.
30. Devindra Kohli, *Kamala Das* (New Delhi: Arnold Heinemann, 1975) 35.
31. David. M. Robinson, "Margaret Fuller and the Transcendental Ethos, Woman in the Nineteenth Century," *PMLA*, 97, January 1982.
32. Tejinder Singh, "Images of Indian Woman," *Perspectives of Kamala Das's Prose*, ed. Iqbal Kaur, 126.
33. Frank O'Connor, *The Lonely Voice: A Study of the Short Story* (London: Macmillan, 1965).
34. Jameela Begum, "Female Consciousness and the Short Story Form," *Perspectives on Kamala Das's Prose*, ed. Iqbal Kaur, 41.
35. Helene Cixous, "The Laugh of Medusa," trans. Keith Cohen and Paula Cohen, *New French Feminism*, ed. Elaine Marks (New York: Schockin, 1981) 245.
36. Iqbal Kaur, *Untying and Retying the Text: An Analysis of Kamala Das's "My Story"* (New Delhi: Bahri, 1990).
37. Rashmi Talwar, *Woman's Space: The Mosaic World of Margaret Drabble and Nayantara Sahgal* (New Delhi: Creative, 1997) 104.
38. Carlos P. Christ and Charlene Spretnak, "Images of Spiritual Power in Women's Fiction" in The Politics of Women's Spirituality (Anchor/ Doubleday, 1982) 239.
39. Chaman Nahal, "Feminism in English Fiction: Forms and Variations," *Feminism and Recent Fiction in English*, ed. Sushila Singh, 31.

The "New Woman" Concept

Kamala Das and the New Indian Woman

The 'New Woman' had its origin in the west and can be traced right from the plays of Shakespeare and Shaw. Shakespeare's heroines like Olivia, Rosalind, and Shaw's Candida are all images of the new woman in English literature. This portrayal of the liberated woman gained popularity down the ages through the women writers and its forerunners were Jane Austen, the Bronte sisters, and George Eliot. Feminist Sarah Grand commented as follows about the new woman in her article "The Brawling Brotherhood" published in *The North American Review* in March 1984:

> Both the cow-women and the scum-women are well within the range of the comprehension of Brawling Brotherhood, but the new woman is a little above them and he has never thought of looking up to where she has been sitting apart in silent contemplation.[1]

The concept of the 'New Woman,' and her definition of self-identity, spelling a refreshing break from the mythological stereotype image of the past, was introduced into the Indian English literature in the post-Independence era. The word 'New Woman' has come to signify a new definition and meaning to the selfhood of woman with a strong realization about her individuality and merit. In the words of Ellen E. Jordan:

> The new woman with her hostility to men, her questioning of marriage, her determination to escape restrictions of home life and her belief that education could make woman capable of leading a financially self-sufficient, single and yet fulfilling life.[2]

This projection of the New Woman was pioneered in Indian English literature by Kamala Das in her verse and extended into her prose works too. The image of Indian woman even a couple of decades ago was different. Woman were bound to a number of restrictions and many boundaries were set and her freedom curtailed by patriarchal ideologies. Literature too was not exempted; hence the women characters in the fictions of women writers were by and large those with mythical pretence. Social inhibitions also prevented writers to bare their minds in public, hence they wedged to the archetypes. It was during this period that Kamala Das dared to expose the crude realities of society and its treatment and outlook towards woman. Das through her writings tried to reveal the extent to which a woman can go, for the fulfilment of her desires and realization of her selfhood. This new portrayal of the Indian woman who were previously typecast only in the mould of Sita-Savitri-Sati by other literary artists saw a new presentation by Das. It is this static, conformist depiction of the Indian woman that Das has confronted and defied, candidly and outrightly.

The discovery of the self and the assertion of selfhood was a new revival of the Indian womanhood. Das according to critics stands synonymous with Indian Renaissance. European Renaissance persuaded people to explore distant world while Indian Renaissance led Indians to delve deep into their own self. This concept that was evolved in the Indian English fictions of Kamala Das transcended all the barriers of culture, tradition and patriarchy. Her women personas were restless individuals, struggling to acquire and establish a distinct identity in the traditionally male-dominated society. Das voices through her protagonists, women's fervent protest against the absurd constraints forced on them and insists on the need for an independent individuality for the Indian womanhood. In *An Introduction*, Das portrays the forceful traits that society enforces on womanhood:

> Dress in sarees, be girl

> Be wife they said. Be embroiderer, be a cook,
> Be a quarreller with servants. Fit in. Oh,
> Belong, cried the categorizers. Don't sit
> On walls or peep in through our lace-draped windows.[3]

But Das redefines all these old archetypes and establishes the bold new woman who defies patriarchy's norms and asserts her selfhood.

> I wore a shirt and my
> Brother's trousers, cut my hair short and ignored
> My womanliness.[4]

After examining Das's short stories published under the title *Padmavati, the Harlot and Other Stories* in the previous chapter, it has been made clear that woman's quest of selfhood has been the major governing theme of Kamala Das's fictional works. Her struggle for freedom and individuality for womanhood made itself clearly heard through various characters. The female characters that Das draws out in her fiction are radical, self-aware and self-conscious individuals, sensitive about their rights. Her characters on realizing that they are subdued and exploited by society, resist and fight back to assert their individuality and ascertain their privileges. This new portrayal of Indian women, who have steadily grown out of their passive acceptance of subjugation and sacrifice to an active being seeking personal gratification and self-fulfilment, is an illustration of positive development and self-realization.

This effort to rouse the Indian woman from their age-long submissiveness, inspiring them to rewrite the old norms with new ideals and principles is well depicted in Das's fiction. She encourages woman to shed inhibitions and make an effort to reveal her self and capabilities. She instigated and in a way challenged Indian women to write openly about themselves, their life and problems without hesitation or inhibition. Das emphasized the importance of woman's role in redrafting her life and building a new environment for herself and for achieving this Das promoted the same notion that Rosalind Brackenbury advocated:

> Nobody writes in a vacuum, away from the political and social structures in which we live. We breathe the air of today's thought, we digest it in everything we read and consider, also, we create it. This is largely the role of women today: to create, present and consider a new world.[5]

This chapter will analyze women characters in two of Das's prominent stories "A Doll for the Child Prostitute"[6] and *Alphabet of Lust*,[7] juxtaposing it with her real life experiences and outlook, as mentioned in her autobiography *My Story*.[8] This evaluation will help confirm that Das has been one of the pioneers who laid the edifice for the 'New Indian Woman' in the Indian English fictional scenario. Also, Manasi, the protagonist of *Alphabet of Lust* will be contrasted with Kamala Das in her autobiography *My Story* to relate and justify that Manasi is an extension of Kamala Das's persona.

Women characters in "A Doll for the Child Prostitute"

The heinous crime of sexual harassment of women and young girls including children is brought out in this story. The precarious state of women and female children is boldly depicted by Das and shocking revelations of the crime are exposed. The writer has also tried to delve deep into the life of these unfortunate women to present a close view of their dreams and aspirations. Their profound desire for independence and identity has been well sketched to depict the basic need of freedom for human beings.

A Doll for the Child Prostitute deals with the world of the young and child prostitutes, who are forced into the flesh trade under various circumstances. and who ardently wish to escape the situation they are caught in. Das, as K.R.S. Iyengar rightly states, "is a fiercely feminine sensibility that dares without inhibitions to articulate the hurts it has received in an insensitive, largely man-made world."[9]

She vigorously articulates about the hypocrisies of society which worship woman as goddess on one hand and on the other, trade her as an object of sexual gratification. She ironically names her victims after the goddesses who are worshipped by men for goodness and prosperity. Sita, Rukmani, Radha, Meera, Saraswati etc. are the names that Das uses. She names the two women who run the brothels as Kaushalya, mythically associated with virtuousness and sacrifice and Lachmibai (Ayee) the goddess of prosperity.

Kamala Das in this story has exposed through her various characters man's outlook and behaviour with woman. A woman is looked upon only as object of flesh and not as an individual being with a mind and soul. Men who come to the brothels make no discretion, neither of age nor status. Their overwhelming greed and lust for sex surpasses their ability of thinking and discerning their acts as moral or immoral. The policeman old enough to be Rukmani's grandfather, wishes to keep the thirteen-year-old as his mistress. By using the persona of a policeman Das puns at the entire police department who are employed for the safety and security of the people and to check the criminal and illegal happenings in society. The Inspector Sahib, a representative of the police force, is himself a regular visitor to the brothel and thereby a part of this unlawful activity. He uses his power to safeguard Ayee, the brothel owner and in turn enjoys free and unrestricted access to the place. This compels Das to questions the very integrity and commitment of the police department to protect this susceptible and exploited section of society. She also comments that it is the men from the higher echelons of society who come to the prostitutes because they have money but no morals. The main women personas in the story are Meera, Sita, Saraswati, Radha, Rukmani and Ayee. All these characters strive to establish their individuality at some stage or the other in the course of the story.

Meera is the most beautiful and educated among the group. She longs for a normal family life of husband and children. Her hopes and wishes find culmination in the young college guy who visits her regularly saving his pocket money. She is obsessed with him and dreams of being his lawfully wedded wife. Her thoughts are expressed in her conversation with the little girl Rukmani where she professes of being his wife: "Yes, he is my husband. He is called Krishna. Is that not strange Rukmani?" Mira asked the little girl. "Is it not strange that I am Meera and he is Krishna." (32-33) Mira secretly marries and elopes with him to start a fresh life that she had longed for ardently. This act of her depicts her longing to free herself from the ignominious shackles of physical trade and thereby establish herself as a new and independent individual. Her wishes get a rude jolt when the lover betrays his promise to protect and safeguard her just a week after their marriage, leaving her with no option but to return back to same old abhorred world of prostitution.

A similar quest for independence is found in the character of the fifteen-year old Sita who too wishes for a family life and motherhood but despises men and sex. Her hatred towards men and sex but love for motherhood and children finds expression in her conversation with Rukmani: "I would love to have a home of my own and a few children. I want him to smile at me and call me Ma. But I don't want to have any men in my house." (64) Her personality finds affirmation in her thoughts where she wants to have no men in her life. This feeling of revulsion is developed as a result of her fear of the male and their sexual hunger, which she has experienced in the brothel. Sita's dreams find association with the new scientific methods of impregnation and birth through test-tube babies. Even Sita's dream for a happy life is suddenly put to a halt when a forceful and unhygienic abortion is conducted on her frail body and she dies as a result.

The character of Saraswati has been one of practical assertiveness. Her understanding and coming to terms with her predicaments helps her face the life of a harlot daringly and without embarrassment. She realizes that as a prostitute, emotion and sentiments have no significance in her life and it is only earnestness in her work that will fetch the rewards. She accepts her work with dignity and performs her job in a well sketched out mechanical manner. She attracts her customers with obscene gestures and accepts all kinds of men who come to her door without any fuss. She treats all her customers in the same unattached fashion and is bothered only about doing her work in the best possible way and fetching the recompense. She is a cool detached type of character who brings the largest income to the house.

Radha, another inmate of the brothel, in spite of being a matter-of-fact person, has some sort of frustration at the situation she is in. Her discontent in being treated secondary to Meera finds vents through her frequent bad temperament. The dialogue of Sita when she introduces Rukmani to Radha gives a glimpse of her, "She is Radha. She has a bad temper. So be careful when you deal with her." (69)

Her conversation with Ayee makes clear her attitude and approach towards her work and her identity, which she accepts without remorse. "You do not like the word prostitute, but you know well that all of us are prostitutes. I believe in being frank and truthful." (73)

Rukmani is also a naive and innocent little girl who is sold to Ayee by her own mother for money. She has already tasted the bitterness of sex as she is raped by her stepfather. The pathetic and pitiable state of this minor is the central theme of the story. Rukmàni represents millions of innocent children who are employed in this trade, who are totally ignorant and uninformed of the corrupt sexual world of the adults. Their youthful purity is shown when Rukmani who wishes to play with a doll in turn becomes a live toy in the hands of sexually greedy men who enjoy to play with her body. The Inspector Sahib who is a regular guest and quite old is enthralled with the thirteen-year-old and wishes to have her as his mistress. The little girl who has no idea of the corrupt world of sex and lust figures in the old man the image of her father, whose love she craves for. She wishes to possess a doll and expresses the desire for the same to the old policeman who she feels is like her father and starts addressing him "Papa." In this kind of a presentation, Das tries to create an embarrassment to the men in society who forget their age, status and identity when they see dejected and abandoned women and girls and pounce upon them with an irresistible sexual hunger. They need to be brought back to their senses by exposing the naked truth and giving them rude jolts. This is what Rukmani does when she calls him "Papa," making him realize his age and position.

Ayee is a mixture of sternness and sensitivity. She loves her girls and treats them with care and caution. She feeds them with healthy food and clothes them well, being sensitive about their needs. At the same time, she scolds them for not being sincere to their work. Her own bitter experiences in life have driven her to this world of prostitution and she wishes eagerly to see her son who left her ten years ago, realizing that she is a harlot. Her open-mindedness finds mention in her wanting to marry Meera to her son: "I shall certainly marry her off to him." (101)

Das's women never forego life, but fight to sustain themselves. They are bold and frank and at times full of frustration and mockery when she highlights and lashes at the male supremacy and women's unprotesting acceptance. The gusto with which Das relates her characters shows her insight and sympathy towards the women who are caught in this work and cannot free themselves. Their burning desire for independence and identity finds mention in different parts of the story. Rukmani comments, "I am not a whore." Sita's wish to be educated which finds mention in her conversation with Rukmani, "Then you must read out a book a client left for me to read. . . . I pretended I was educated and so he gave me that book." (71-75)

Mira's wish to get married and settle down is an example of these women's desire to have an individuality of their own. Das has effectively used the truncated novel i.e., the story form to express the fractured female identity that struggles to break out of various constraints they are placed in the male-dominated world.

The central theme that Das has tried to portray through all these characters in the story, is their desperate need to establish an independent identity in hostile surroundings that they are caught in. These prostitutes either by means of escaping or by accepting their work try to find a place for themselves in society. A wishful longing for return to a respectable position and a normal life can be seen in each of these characters. The problem and outlook about prostitution acquires a new dimension in this story. Das draws attention to how this socio-cultural problem can be solved through the change in attitude of Lachmibai and the police Inspector. At the same time, Das also calls for a change in individual attitude and approach.

Manasi in *Alphabet of Lust*

In her first long story titled *Alphabet of Lust* (1976), running into 148 pages, Das has tried to "challenge the accepted notions of the female and redraft general opinion on the feminine mystique"[10] by making her protagonist emphasize her self and develop into a bold and brazen individual. Manasi stands as the representative of the New Indian woman in the story and Das has effectively tried to develop the protagonist into a new and forceful individual.

Manasi the famed poetess had been married in haste to Amol Mitra, a struggling Government official much senior to her. Das portrays her as a young, vibrant and attractive lady, desired by many young and influential men in society, but she is forced to marry a mismatched person by her parents: "She was still attractive. Her mind was active and very much alive. She was admired by the young as a revolutionary poetess." (17)

The dawn of self-realization and self-worth in Manasi draws a new selfhood and from this point, Das has sketched the growth of her character from self-alienation to self-assertion. Manasi who is described as living a peaceful and contended life with her husband and daughter till the arrival of Vijay Raje into their life, in fact indicates Manasi's estrangement from her individual self. This withdrawal from an active life to that of self-seclusion was a result of her lost identity, resulting from the death of her fiancé. The unexpected loss of her dreams and her lover made Manasi alienate herself from life. With the coming of Vijay Raje in the picture, Das delineates the growth of Manasi from self-isolation to self-identification. This can be understood from her initial grappling in submitting to Raje's advances, to her final acceptance of his offer to spend a week with him in Simla. She decides to accept his offer, not just for a pair of diamond earrings, which he promises. Looking into the future of this relationship she judges the advantages she can get and it is the temptation for power and position that attracts her to him. Her self-imposed isolation soon fades away with her startling discovery that she loves life and its exuberance. Her overwhelming desire to live and her recognition for an urge for liberation from the self-isolation finds expression in her sudden change of attitude. The deep-rooted and suppressed desires of Manasi's life find reappearance when she receives the coveted Padma Bhushan award with the political influence of Vijay Raje. Her hidden desires for fame and money spring up and in this process of her 'individuation,' Manasi, steps out of her isolated life and moves towards self-assertion.

Manasi is portrayed as the symbol of the new liberated Indian woman, who is shrewd and clever. On realizing that Vijay

Raje is the ladder with which she can comprehend her ambitions, she decides to make use of the man to achieve her goal. A searing realization emerges and she reaches the conclusion that wisdom lies not in declining the offer of Vijay Raje but in making the journey worth the sacrifice. In surrendering to his wishes, Manasi prices her self-esteem by making use of Raje for attaining fame and fortune—the peak position in the country's management. Das has thus reversed the order of patriarchy. It is usually the men who employ women for the achievements of their ambition, and discard them once they achieve their ends, but here Das reverses the action. In the story *Alphabet of Lust*, Manasi is the one who makes her choice of men to rise to power and realize her ambitions. "I rented out my body for a pair of diamond earrings. And hereafter for power I shall rent it out to the most influential tenant I can hope to get." (41)

By re-writing the archetype woman in the character of Manasi, Kamala Das who is aware of the ramification of sexual oppression has tried to revolt against it vehemently. She tries to establish the fact that it is the unequal social system of society that is responsible for the social exploitation and isolation of the women folk. She strongly feels that it is only by rebelling against the patriarchal norms that women will be noticed and their voice heard. It is worth remembering what Simone de Beauvoir has commented in her book *The Second Sex*:

> One is not born, but rather becomes, a woman. No biological, psychological, or economic fate determines the figure that the human female presents in society; it is civilization as a whole that produces this creature, intermediate between male and eunuch, which is described as feminine.[11]

Manasi's intellectual assertion stands as symbols of the self-conscious new Indian woman, who steps out of her traditional bondage, creating a new set of ideals for herself. The tragedy that befell Manasi with the death of her fiancé, her illegitimate pregnancy out of the relationship and the hasty marriage to an inappropriate man, led her to self-alienation. Her marriage to Amol Mitra who looked old enough to be her father makes her life totally despondent. Her marriage is a loveless and emotionless relationship and her hopelessness finds expression in the following: "We are not suited to each other. He is busy with his files all the time. I like people, conversation, some show of affection." (10) Her poems were born out of her desolation, which finds mention in the following lines: "But then she would not have been a poetess, for her poetry had burst out of the mire of utter hopelessness like a red lotus." (9)

Manasi's true spirits surface as soon as she realizes about her ambitions in life, and finds a source that can help realize her ambitions. Her quest for self-assertion is so overpowering that Manasi recognizes no impediments, no inhibitions, no ethical or social code. She decides once and for all not to put the opportunity at stake and resolves to utilize it at all costs. There is no retreat or repentance once her goals are set and the path selected, for which she has to sacrifice a lot. Das portrays Manasi as one who is ready to stoop in order to conquer, which is a sign of the newfound approach of women as a means of self-realization and accomplishment.

There is a marked change in the portrait of Indian woman, which Kamala Das draws through the character of Manasi. She is not one of the self-sacrificing and altruistic women, who considers herself an object of possession; instead she is a blatant and boisterous person who is all set to realize her aspirations in life. She aims at being the subject and authority of her selfhood and not be content with a marginalized position in the world of masculine hierarchies. Manasi alters the existing social structures and creates a rightful place as a significant person and part of society. She breaks the old patterns of docility and complacency, which Simone de Beauvoir had commented: "Women do not set themselves up as subject and hence have erected to virile myth in which their projects are reflected; they still dream through the dreams of men." (174)

She is extremely ambitious and power possessed, hence she ventures into politics, a field, under the monopoly of men breaking up the power structure of male dominance. The shift in women's outlook is another point depicted through Manasi's political ambition. Stepping out of the domestic arena and being an active participant in world affairs, is another aspect that the new Indian women have started becoming conscious about. Manasi comprehends the need of political power and authority for achieving her ambitions, rising high in life and winning fame, money and recognition.

Kamala Das has in the persona of Manasi tried to expose to the world the social, moral, and political corruption that takes place and how women are made the object of men's bait. This is also a hint in extenuating Manasi's ambition and her dealings with men. Raje who is a corrupt man decides to exploit Manasi's beauty and body, to secure his political position; Krishnan assists him in getting beautiful women from all parts of the land and offers to the lustful men in power. This is an indication to the fact that women are treated as objects of sex by men and thrown away after use. Those who fall prey in this game of sex and politics are Stella, an orphan, Sita, the dancer and others. These women, since they lacked power, position and money, could neither defend themselves nor fight back. It is under the realm of this corrupt society and men whose easy victims are powerless and socially weak women, that Manasi's yearning for power and money is justified. Comprehending Raje's motives in using her for his own ends, makes Manasi play the game to her advantage. This desire to reach the peak of authority from where she can assert herself and also protect her being, is achieved at the cost of forfeiting her family and her body, satiating the lust of the men in power.

She is portrayed as the spokesperson of the frail and vulnerable women who have no strength and guts to fight back, and whose voice is muted because power lies in the hands of these very men who have abused her. Stella, who is killed by Vijay Raje, is an apt example of the same.

It is on understanding the potency that power and politics provides that inspires Manasi to bid for it. It is this intellectual realization of the need of authority in the country's framework that finds expression through her character. Das thus endorses and promotes this new political and intellectual awakening among women as the only way to redress their problems and resolve their issues.

The concept of physical and sexual affirmation of women, their physical desires and search for sexual fulfilment also finds expression in the character of Manasi. Sex with her husband for Manasi was "an act of self-mortification." (16) Manasi on discovering her love for life and self, decides to rework her thoughts and actions. She liberates herself from the concepts of chastity of the traditional Indian wife, and her self-identification leads her to discover a new identity in her. Manasi's married and sexual life is full of discontent, and she longs to live her life on her own terms. Manasi longs not for her husband's intellectual praise; instead, she wishes to be admired and acclaimed for her physical beauty:

> She wanted him to praise the contours of her full breasts and the smooth silk of her thighs. She wanted him to smother her with surprise gifts which had no utility value. Instead he bought for her tins of ovaltine or a bottle of pickles picking them up at some reduction sale and offering them to her heraldically as though they were coveted trophies. (27)

Manasi refuses to be treated merely as an object for male sexual gratification, and has her own desires of sexual fulfilment. Manasi's reversion from her husband's sexual advancements finds mention in the following extract:

> Don't touch me tonight, she hissed. This is all that you want from me, this activity on the bed. How I wish you turn impotent. I hate the sight of you. I bear this suffering only out of a sense of gratitude. After all, you feed me, don't you? (15)

This bold and blatant protest is uncommon in an Indian wife. Das speaks through the persona of Manasi, woman's personal desire for sex. She emphasizes that sex is not the domain of men alone, and that women too have their moods and preferences for it. Manasi's longing for sexual assertion acts as a spur to her acceptance of the overture of the young and handsome Vijay Raje. Her dreams and wishes find voice in her comment, "We would have made an excellent pair: poetess and politician." (15) This thought is brought out when Manasi willingly surrenders herself to Vijay Raje's sexual advances and enjoys the same.

> There was an ache in her breasts which only his red lips would satisfy. Was it lust? She asked herself. Was she waking to sexual desire which never in her life she had experienced? The exact centre of her body was in a whirl. (32)

Manasi is a shrewd character who utilizes the very same men who use her for their physical hunger, by taking advantage of their weakness for her. She willingly surrenders to their carnal desires and uses it as a ladder to climb to the top position of the country's power. On realizing that Vijay Raje was the icon of power politics, and also a close associate of the Prime Minister, and knowing his lust for her, she accepts his offer to share the hotel room with him in Simla. Her intention is to kill two birds with one arrow. Making use of Raje's association with the P.M. and exploiting the opportunity she gets to spend time alone in his company, she cleverly allows the P.M. to make physical overtures to her. Manasi's candid and liberal conferring of sexual favours upon those who matter is a part of her quest for identity. Very tactfully by pleasing the P.M. she is able to find a place for herself first in the upper house of the parliament and then slowly she carves her way to the top, pushing out of her path all those who stand as obstructions. Raje, whose plan was to employ Manasi for his political security and be in the good books of the Prime Minister, fails to realize Manasi's brilliant moves. She plays her game like a skilled chess master and beats Raje in his own game. Her sexual surrender to all those whom she believes wield great power and influence causes no remorse of conscience in her, so long as she is sure that they will assist her climb socially and politically. As she remarks: "I am willing to do whatever the P.M. wants me to do. It is not as if I am a chaste woman now. A *pativrata*. You saw to it that I became a mere tart." (40-41)

Finally she wins the game and inflicts revenge upon him by grabbing the Prime Ministership from Vijay Raje, which was what she had aimed at. All that she had lost and sacrificed in this journey for power was willingly done. Though she has sacrificed quite a bit in this quest for power, the final victory soothes the wounds and she is content. Manasi's quest and assertion of her physical individuality eventually yields results bringing her to the premier position of power, success and glory.

Kamala Das's Self-Assertion in *My Story*

Das's self-discovery and self-assertion in *My Story* is developed from an unhappy married life leading to a forceful isolation from her true self. She is trapped in the disgusting and dissonant confusion of a new life that was forced on her in the marriage with Madhav Das. Though she had no desire for Mr. Das, she had to consent for the same and her state of desperation finds mention in the following lines: "after my engagement I became moody and my mind clouded over with doubts. Had I been reckless in accepting the proposal?" (82)

Das's longing for a genuine consideration and love, which she had never received from her parents, was denied to her in married life. About this, Kamala Das remarks:

> I had expected him to take me in his arms and stroke my face, my hair, my hands and whisper loving words. I had expected him to be all that I wanted my father to be, and my mother. I wanted conversation, companionship and warmth. Sex was far from my thoughts. (84)

The forceful sexual encounter by her husband that she had to endure unwillingly is drawn out thus: "without warning he fell on me, surprising me by the extreme brutality of the attack. I tried unsuccessfully to climb out of his embrace. . . . Again and again throughout that unhappy night he hurt me." (90)

Das records her initiation into sexual intercourse via marital rape, which is a common experience of many Indian women. The explanation that Das provides is that of sexual violence and licensed rape that husbands inflict on their wives. The consequences of this sex-perverted attitude of her husband with no thought for her makes Das decide to be disloyal to him, at least bodily. This was in a way, her mode to avenge the indifferent attitude of her husband and thereby assert her physical self. Her hunting for love outside marriage was not for sexual gratification but for an emotional oneness, understanding and companionship where the union of body was not what she desired but that of the mind that she craved.

At the close of the autobiography, Das describes how after she was well established as a writer, she was constantly propositioned by strangers and even by male friends who had read her works and concluded that she was an easily available person. Das at this point asserts that, "Sex did not interest me except as a gift I could grant my husband to make him happy." (213) Iqbal Kaur comments as follows, "I would like to repeat that it is not lust or sex or carnal hunger but rather an escape from all this that drags her from man to man."[12] She was unaffected by the people and society who resented her conduct and manners, and had the courage to assert herself fighting all odds. Her infidelity is a way of her questioning the sexual liberties that man takes so much for granted. Das was unlike the Indian woman who meekly took to orders, obeying and confining to the man-made rules of subjectivity. Her attempts have always been to redefine the marginalization of woman by an assertive and self-determined behaviour. She makes herself clear as a person, "developing independently, like sturdy shoots of the banyan growing out of crevices in the walls of ancient fortresses." (77) Das could never stand the captivity of the woman by the patriarchy and strongly retaliated to it. Das believed:

> A social system which produces such a binary opposition of masculine and feminine, and so rigidly structures men and women into these positions, promises only the ironic collapse of communication, misunderstanding, frustrated desire, and pathological incompleteness.[13]

She found an outlet for establishing her individuality through her writings. In this manner her selfhood, which was too strong to be defeated, got transcended in her writings. All that she could not achieve in factual life was transcended into her fiction where her protagonist voiced her silent cries in the form of abrasive violent outbursts. Through her writing Das tried to break down the existing social power structures and create a new world for women. Gail Chester and Sigrid Nielson had declared in their feminist essay as follows: "Writing plays a vital part in forming our perceptions of our lives as women, in working out our feminist views and in communicating them to others."[14]

It can be ascertained that Das was successful in establishing a new order of feminine personas, in the Indian English fiction; one of the most closely resembling characters to Das's individual person, being that of Manasi in *Alphabet of Lust*.

Reflections

After examining "A Doll for the Child Prostitute" and *Alphabet of Lust*, it can be well understood that the characters and incidents that are referred in these stories are mainly drawn from

Das's personal experiences and has ample semblance to the autobiographical sketches found in *My Story*. In short, Das seems to have dredged up the diverse incidents of her life in her fiction. As K. Meera Bai writes: "A writer is apt to be more sensitive to the disturbing day-to-day happenings and changes around him, and tends to react and respond intensely. He creates a world of his own depending upon the angle from which he views the world. The works, more often than not, contain and reflect the experience and vision of their creator."[15]

Das's sincere concern about the problem of prostitution that finds mention in her story "A Doll for the Child Prostitute," seems to have stemmed from the incidents she had witnessed in her own family and society, which find reference in her autobiography *My Story*. There is the mention of the kitchen maid of Nalapat who was dismissed from work by the grandmother knowing that one of the family members was taking interest in her. Another similar incident is about the "ignorant and innocent" girl Kunhukutty, the maidservant of Nalapat who is raped and mutilated by men. She sympathizes with these unfortunate women who are subjected to the physical torture by men and the defiler of her chastity always goes scot-free. The victimized is the one who suffers by being labelled as "an immoral woman" and she carries this stigma with her throughout her life. Her 'militant and blunt' voice against this sexual exploitation finds forceful illustration in many of her literary works and "A Doll for the Child Prostitute" is one such forceful story, which is also an eye opener to society.

Similarly the secondary position given to woman and her physical and psychological exploitation, both in her family and in society is contested by Das in her story *Alphabet of Lust*. Manasi's basic life and happenings have resemblance with Das's life as mentioned in *My Story*. Though not wholly autobiographical, the author seems to seek a garb in the being of Manasi Mitra, in order to give vent to her thoughts and express her views more candidly and forcefully. Das's eminently personal thought and experiences find an outlet and manifestation through the persona of Manasi. Right from the event of her marriage to a mismatched man Mr. Amol Mitra to Manasi's experiences in the ominous world of politics, sexual love, physical exploitation and betrayal are extended expressions born out of her personal life. Similarly to Manasi, Das in her autobiography, *My Story*, speaks of herself as an ordinary good girl from the society's standards and it was deprivation of love and understanding that turned her into a rebel. If Kamala Das and Manasi had a loving and caring man as husband, they would not have been what they turned out to be. A love-lorn childhood and adolescence coupled with an emotionally deprived married life made them break away from the self-yielding attitude to that of self-identification and self-affirmation. It is after a long duration of self-surrender and subjugation to their husband's sexual desires and wants that Kamala Das and Manasi determine to give priority to their needs and desires. They step out of the sacrosanct of marriage and decide to be "unfaithful to him, at least physically" (95) to pacify their own burning desire for love and revenge. This approach is unusual and unexpected of an Indian woman and Das has bluntly defied the age-old Indian attitude of self-denial and self-annihilation of the women folk. It can be recollected that Das too had opted for political power and contested elections.

Das portrays women being exploited by the politically powerful to satisfy their lust and as objects of gift to men in order to remain in power depicting the contempt and dishonour of society towards the women community. Both Das and Manasi have been puppets in the hands of family and society. Living a discontented and frustrated life, both decide to do away with their passivity and express themselves as active independent individuals of flesh and blood. On realizing their selves, their needs and aspirations, both these women determinedly explore their life and leave no stones unturned to achieve happiness and fulfilment of their self.

The other female characters of the story like Stella, Sita, Suparna and even the protagonist herself, are exploited and physically abused by men for their lust and needs. Das deals with this theme of sexual violence with tremendous dexterousness and presents to the world the physical, mental and psychological trauma that the victims undergo. Das's infuriation finds recourse in her rebellious expressions and unconventional attitude that she and her women characters resort to in factual life and fiction. Das's equation of life with art on one-to-one basis is well depicted in *Alphabet of Lust*. While Kamala Das tries to assert her individuality and exposes her desires through the medium of her writing, Manasi does it on a more open and public level.

Das's treatment of the new woman, in her fictional works and her autobiography created discord in the Indian literary circle and raised a lot of eyebrows. It was by exploring her own sense of identity—for writing autobiographically becomes in part public performance—Das powerfully redefined her own life, laying down the identity of the New Indian Woman. To Das her writings came as an exploration and discovery of her own identity, and as Joseph Conrad puts it,

> In truth every novelist must begin by creating for himself a world great or little in which he can honestly believe. This world cannot be made otherwise than in his own image.[16]

Das set the example herself of a new awakened woman, before campaigning forthe same through her writings. Das's works speak of her determined protest against patriarchal norms and practices that oppress woman and for her courage in continuously mining her own life experiences for material. Thus, much of this feminist championing of Das was intended as a corrective to the mainstream, masculinist reading

Contention

In the general parlance, the outlook of Kamala Das and her ideologies of the new woman may not completely be approved by society. But a new perspective through which both Manasi's and Das's character can be viewed and justified is that both took to their independent ways as an outlet to the irrepressible and immensely pent-up desire for freedom and authority. Their decisions and the methods adopted to acquire all that they prized so immensely, in fact, spring from the anger, rage and rebellion of a woman struggling to assert her individuality of body and mind. Their suppression, exploitation and defeat at the hands of men compel them to break the rules and turn defiant. In a society of male prerogatives, the only way to succeed from their point of view is by playing the game as men play and hitting back at the right time when opportunity knocks. This outlook leads to making use of any and every source that comes their way, which will help them reach their destination. The self eventually asserts through the uncharacteristic and the aberrant ways with the rational manifesting in the irrational.

It can finally be said that through Manasi, the identity of the writer merges with the identity of the art. Das and Manasi, both refuse to submerge their entity, and revolt against the customary instructions for women to obey the dictates of men. Both are strong-willed and self-determined women and their bearing against the hierarchal rules of patriarchy is indomitable. Their questioning spirit repudiates the old norms leading their quest to the evolution of a new personality, with self-acclaimed principles. Both Das and Manasi are seen to practice their own faith and live on the provisos that they set down for themselves. They do not allow the betrayals, and disappointments of life to bog them down, instead the emotional ruins and sexual defeats make them strong to rise up and embark on a quest for self-fulfilment. Insisting on being their true self, they succeed in discovering their selfhood even in the midst of all kinds of pressures, mounted by the entrenched patriarchal values.

It can also be contended that Manasi is a prolonged extension of Das's mental framework. *My Story* follows Kamala Das's life from the age of four; through her sexual awakening, an early and seemingly disastrous marriage, extra-marital affairs, the birth of her three children, her growing literary career and finally it draws out to a slow but steady coming to terms with her spouse, writing, and sexuality. Das's journey through the autobiography is a movement from revolt to conformity, which ends in surrender and acceptance of her life. But in portraying Manasi, Das has gone a step further. Manasi, who starts her quest for identity and assertion of her individuality, from a similar plane as Das, does not give up until she reaches her desired goal of power, in spite of the tremendous hardships and defeats she faces.

Das seems to have in the persona of Manasi of the story *Alphabet of Lust*, fought it out with the masculine powers, as a completion of her own quest for assertion. Das had crossed the boundaries of marriage in search of true love, but she found all of them possessed with the myth of male-sovereignty. Each of them tried to extract from her their wants, but could never return her unadulterated and unconditional love. Her search for "an ideal lover" had failed; and this leads her to a more frustrated state of mind. It is this frustration and search for autonomy and assertion of a woman that finds expression in the character of Manasi. Through Manasi, Das brings the new Indian woman forcefully to life and views the social structure of the country from a feminine eye, and challenges its established systems of governance. By having relations with men outside marriage, Das actually tries to challenge the sexual politics and the very basis of male supremacy.

Both Das and Manasi avenge the men who exploit them mentally and physically by being unconcerned and unfaithful towards them. Das's revenge first with her father, the man who compelled her into marriage without taking her consent into consideration and then her husband who neglected her and sexually exploited her for his carnal lust, made Das feel hurt and miserable. Manasi too, like Das, was forcefully married off to the wrong man by her family and it had made her dispirited, forcing her to succumb to her fate. Vijay Raje who entered her life as a relief also exploited her weakness and contributed in aggravating her pain and vengeance towards men and society. It was as a result of all this that Das and Manasi turned rebels and retaliated in an unconventional way.

It was an act of confrontation and not a means to escape reality. Manasi is an expansion of Das's being which she has tried to sketch. In one of her interviews, Kamala Das states:

> I wanted to make women of my generation feel that if men could do something wrong they could do it themselves too. I wanted them to realize that they were equal. I wanted to remove the gender difference. I wanted to see that something happened to the society which had such strong inhibitions and which only told lies.[17]

Das shunned falsity and took up the task of accurately representing life in general and women's predicament in particular in its truest form. She ruminates on women's issues in India where even after attaining independence, women's education and development was unheard of and marriage was deemed the ultimate goal. And the most befitting ornament and behaviour of women was total silence and total submission to the male authority.

Das's writings emerged from various factors; an untendered and cloistered childhood without maternal care, a turbulent adolescence with a mismatched marriage, appalling conditions of women in the family and society etc. She thus aimed at sketching a sincere and genuine picture of a woman without any artifices. The question that lurked uppermost in Das's mind as a writer was about writing as a woman, and relating to her readers as a woman.

The New Woman image that Das introduced through her writings has often come up for discussion and debate, giving birth to a new stream of consciousness to the other women writers of Indian English literature. The dawn of the Gynocritics—the study of female writers in the context of their own and not in the context of the Great Tradition of their male predecessors and their writings, can be said to have begun in the Indian English literature with the coming of Kamala Das. It can be definitely said that Kamala Das is the first major women writer in Indian English who boldly dealt with what may now be termed as the 'woman question' and presented the Indian womanhood with a new fascia. She is undoubtedly a forerunner to the feminist writers in India who gave a new direction and dimension to Indian woman's identity. The coming of the New Indian woman to the fictional scenario, who presented herself without any guise and unbothered about its consequences, owes its origin to Das's autobiography *My Story*. As Das herself confesses: "This book has cost me many things that I held dear, but I do not for a moment regret having written it."[18]

It was with her open presentation of a woman, her perspectives about her self, her life and her aspirations, that Das asserted her identity and unfurled the message of a new awakening of the Indian women. Her protagonists were mostly rebels and this kind pf protest fiction enabled women writers of her age and her successors to project their anger and frustrations in various forms and expressions. Das heralded a new generation of women writers and urged them towards self-exploration, withdrawing from the male society, and culture, searching for woman's space. Her women characters in all the stories trace their journey from the inner realms of consciousness to the outer realms of discovery and fusion.

It can finally be concluded that Das and her women personas did away with the age-old, custom-ridden ideas and principles nurturing a new generation of womanhood with fresh ideas, hopes and aspirations. The 'New Woman' that Das sketched had a mind and body of her own of which she was the master. These women have a dream in their hearts, of carving a niche for themselves in the world with a quest to have a self-established and an independent identity. The remark of K.C. Srivastava about Kamala Das can be recalled: "Her urge for identity and liberation finds its fruition and fulfilment in the superimposition of her . . . self over her domestic self, in her emergence . . . by overcoming domestic self which compelled her to play the monotonous and enslaved wife and mother."[19]

It can thus be concluded that this "New Woman" image is a result of the self-awareness that has developed among women and Das has tried to propagate and promote it further through her writings. Das too seems to passionately endorse the principle, which Simone de Beauvoir had foreseen way back in the Nineties:

> On the day when it will be possible for woman to love not in her weakness but in her strength, not escape herself but to find herself, not to abase herself but to assert herself—on that day love will become for her, as for man, a source of life and not of mortal danger.[20]

NOTES

1. Meena Shirwadkar, *Images of Woman in the Indo-Anglian Novel* (New Delhi: Sterling, 1979) 56.
2. Ellen E. Jordan, "The Christening of the New Woman," *The Victorian Newsletter* (Spring 1983) 19.
3. Kamala Das, "An Introduction," *Summer in Calcutta* (New Delhi: Everest Press, 1965).
4. *Ibid.*

5. Rosalind Brackenbury, "Women and Fiction: How We Present Ourselves and Others," *In Other Words* (London: Hutchinson) 56.
6. Kamala Das, "A Doll for the Child Prostitute," *Padmavati, the Harlot and Other Stories* (New Delhi: Sterling, 1994).
7. Kamala Das, *Alphabet of Lust* (New Delhi: Orient Paperbacks, 1976).
8. Kamala Das, *My Story* (New Delhi: sterling, 1978).
9. K.R.S. Iyengar, *Indian Writing in English* (New Delhi: Sterling, 1973) 680.
10. Usha V.T "One Woman's Autobiography: Kamala Das's My Story," *Kamala Das A Critical spectrum*, ed. Rajeshwar Mittapalli and Pier Piciucco (New Delhi: Atlantic, 2001) 2.
11. Simone de Beauvoir, *The Second Sex*, 1949 rpt. (London: Picador, 1988) 295.
12. Iqbal Kaur, "Sexual Politics and Kamala Das," *Perspectives in Kamala Das's Prose*, ed. Iqbal Kaur (New Delhi: Intellectual, 1995) 162.
13. Patricia Waugh, *Feminine Fictions: Revisiting the Postmodern* (London: Routledge, 1989) 107-108.
14. Gail Chester and Sigrid Nielson, "Writing as a Feminist," *In Other Words*, 15.
15. K. Meera Bai, *Women's Voices* (New Delhi: Prestige, 1996) 26.
16. *Notes on Life and Letters* (London: Putnam, 1921) 7-8.
17. Interview, 19/08/91, qtd. "Feminist Revolution and Kamala Das's *My Story*" by Iqbal Kaur (Patiala: Century Twenty One Publications, 1992) 139-50.
18. Kamala Das, Preface to *My Story*.
19. K.C. Srivastava, "The Novels of Kamala Das: The Quest for Identity" in *The Indian Novel in English: Essays in Criticism*, ed. R.K. Sinha (Ranchi: Ankit, 1987) 117.
20. Simone de Beauvoir, *The Second Sex*, 679

Kamala Das to Kamala Suraiya: In Pursuit of Self-Exploration

A work of literature in the words of K. Meera Bai, "simply does not state "what is," but suggests by implication "what ought to be."[1] Kamala Das's input to the Indian literature is evidently remarkable as her writings stand out with its singular and forthright representation of Indian woman. Her English fiction, though insignificant quantitatively, reveals a vast spectrum of the oddity and contradictions within the Indian ethos, ideology, culture and outlook of patriarchy towards its women folk.

Her literary work has indisputably established Kamala Das as an excellent writer of effective fiction. Her short stories have been noted for their effective representation of woman's predicament and dilemmas and Das has voiced her opinion strongly in protest against the discrimination meted out to womanhood. The success formula about which she had mentioned in an interview to T.N. Geetha for a good piece of prose work is "poetry, story + magic." This equation seems to have worked wonders in her fictional works and as Das comments, "I see poetry in an experience, and then see good prose coming out of the same experience."[2] On the basis of the English stories of Das that have been studied here, it is evident that Das defies accepting gender-inequality and defends what Gerda Lerner in her book *The Creation of Patriarchy* professes: "to enable women and men to free their minds from patriarchal thought and at least build a world, free of dominance and hierarchy and a world that is truly human."[3] Das not only beckons but also guides the Indian womanhood to develop an identity for her and to refuse blind submission to the society with male prerogatives.

Kamala Das as a writer and as an individual has been in an incessant search for independence and identity, both in her factual and fictional life. Her writings reflect and meditate upon the life and society that she had lived in and her characters and writings are mostly first-hand information drawn up from her life experiences. Thus in all her stories there lies an undertone of autobiographical note, making the situations and characters of her fictions well associable and comprehensible. The characters she sketches in her writings embodies her viewpoint about the image that Indian woman should have. Das's writings substantiate what Helene Cixous remarks:

> I write this as a woman, towards women. When I say 'woman' I'm speaking of woman in her inevitable struggle against conventional man: and of a universal woman subject who must bring women to their senses and to their meaning in history.[4]

She stands out among women writers, in being a person who professes and practises the same principles and philosophies that she advocates in her writings. Das's characters in her fiction and her personality in true-life always went hand in hand and this distinctiveness of Das can be expressed borrowing the lines of Shakespeare from his play *Hamlet*:

> Suit the action to the word, the word to the action; with this special observance, that you o'erstep not the modesty of nature.[5]

Through her fictional works, Das has freely and frankly expressed the need for change in outlook and attitude of both society and family towards woman. She aimed at wiping out the gender inequality that was so deeply rooted in the Indian minds and giving woman her rightful position in society. Das refused to accept defeat and it is this boldness of character and strength of mind that has been sublimated in her characters. She also raised her voice in protest against the unjust treatment of woman and "writing as therapy," for Das "emerged as a significant strategy."[6]

Das tried to create a social awareness of the existing reality and daringly expressed the happenings in society, which hitherto were not referred to or spoken about in public. Her characters are "a mirror of the feminine persona's place within society, an image of the enclosure of its victims"[7] and her themes include various aspects of man-woman relationship, love, lust, sex, exploitation, prostitution, homosexuality, betrayal etc. in all its diverse dimensions. Das fearlessly dared to portray the physical needs and intellectual aspirations of a woman, which were never before paid attention to in the literary writings. She did away with the diffident attitude of woman in discussing their sexual and emotional desires and explicitly wrote about them. This honesty and candidness in her writing earned her a negative image but it laid the edifice of a new branch of writing in Indian English fiction. Das's characters are such that they dare all odds and strive to survive against them. This bold depiction of a revived womanhood came to occupy the centre stage of the literary works of many other writers. Her writing can indisputably be said to have laid the beginning of feminist movement; her writings in the Indian English literature inspired other women writers to take up women's issues seriously in their literary works.

It can undoubtedly be stated that Kamala Das as a writer has been able to move on to a more radical and progressive questioning of values and attitudes upheld through the ages. She has been instrumental in formulating a contemporary consciousness through her English fiction by strongly resisting and subverting traditional patriarchal impositions. As a writer she has taken up the role and responsibility in creating a new pattern of living and thinking for the Indian women.

Das can be ranked among the foremost feminists in Indian English literature. Through her writings she has aimed at both transforming and transcending the prevalent status of woman in society. For Das too, as remarked by Jean-Paul Sartre, literature, a "creative act aims at a total renewal of the world."[8] Das with her skill for writing took up the status of a self-appointed spokesperson of the Indian womanhood and tried to speak for and on behalf of them. Here it is worth remembering P.B. Shelley's view that poets [writers] are the unacknowledged representatives of the human race.

Her feminist consciousness is well portrayed in all her literary works through which she has asserted the impact that literature can bring about in a woman's life. Das's writings attest Pam Morris's analysis about the definitive role of literature in redefining a writer. Morris had commented as follows:

> It has traditionally been believed that creative forms of writing can offer special insight into human experience and sharpen our perception of social reality. Literary texts may therefore provide a more powerful understanding of the ways in which society works to the advantage of women.[9]

Through description and speech, Das vividly brings forth the depth of the situation as in the story "The Little Kitten" where infidelity of the wife becomes a metaphor of revolt against her secondary status. The frequent use of parody is another forceful feature of her stories. This technique helps deliver the stories the required impact and impetus like the title "The Princess of Avanti." Das employs irony to hide the truth, not to deceive but to achieve special symbolic and artistic effect. Similarly satire is used as a tool for denigrating the subject making it ridiculous evoking the feeling of contempt, scorn and indignation. She deliberately abstains from making authorial comments and leaves her reader to evaluate and assess the situation and make their own decisions.

Das's sketches of her women characters explicitly reveal her opinion and outlook. Her diverse women characters are appreciably outstanding as they elicit her efforts to acquire for the Indian woman a new identity, dignity and position in society. She is among the foremost Indian women writers who dared to "crack the mould, and establish an attitude and viewpoint"[10] that the Indian patriarchy was quite unfamiliar with. Her literary personas have depicted the stark realities of life, the sexual exploitation, violence, disrespect and secondary position that a woman in Indian society has to face contrary to the popular belief that women are worshipped in India. The portrayal of such contrary women characters in her stories like "The Princess of Avanti" and "A Doll for the Child Prostitute" not only exhibit the profound sensitive insight of the novelist but also present the seriousness of purpose in her writings.

In her stories like "Darjeeling," "Sanatan Choudhuri's Wife," "December" and "Walls," Das has also depicted characters who are less fierce and submit to a life within the framework of society and marriage. In spite of their gentle temperament, these women too are assertive of their personality and desires, thereby illustrating the fact that acceptance does not mean subservience. Some of her women depict a fierce sense of independence and are extremely sensitive about their assertion of selfhood. They revolt against the old norms and refuse to be cowed down even in the face of adversities: the nameless protagonists in "That Woman," "A Little Kitten," "The Sign of the Lion," and "Iqbal." Manasi in *Alphabet of Lust* and the protagonist in "The Sea Lounge" are representatives of the new Indian woman. They have the fortitude to stand on their own without the support of men and assert their independence and individuality.

Das through her protagonists summons the Indian womanhood to shake out from their self-effacing, self-surrendering attitude and insists on a change in approach towards life. She advocates the process of self-discovery, self-recovery and self-assertiveness, which is the only way Das feels Indian women can build and ascertain her identity and worth.

In spite of all the predicaments and challenges of life, the women characters of Das sooner or later comprehend their individuality and affirm their selfhood. Thus, assertion of identity is undoubtedly the major and most distinguishable feature that Das has presented through her women personas. Das who has been in an incessant pursuit for an independent selfhood for Indian woman has been successful in emerging as a writer instrumental in establishing the New Indian Woman, bold enough to assert her identity. Das can thus be called a paradigm that has consistently and continuously kept making efforts in quest of an authentic existence and selfhood questioning the restrictions exercised on the Indian womanhood. In short it can be concluded that Das has effectively put to action what Mary Warnock had remarked:

> Authentic existence can begin only when we have realized and thoroughly understood what we are. Once we have grasped that human reality is characterized by the fact that each human being is uniquely, himself and no one else of us has his own possibilities to fulfill.[11]

With her conversion to Islam, Kamala Das underwent a change in her persona and outlook towards life. But that undoubtedly was no form of self submission. Instead it was a new journey in search of a new identity. Her outlook and approach towards life (as recorded in the interview in the last chapter, immediately after her conversion) reveals that she believed in experiencing and experimenting life in all its facets. Suraiya relied on her personal findings and instincts and therefore constantly pursued the path of self-exploration and revival. She had never blindly acknowledged what others thought or believed and this spirit of hers once again echoed with her conversion. Even in her conversion, she had been true to her identity and beliefs. She had always lived life on her own terms and the conversion once again proved her form of self manifestation and self-determination. In her new journey as Kamala Suraiya, her views about women found more concrete facets and variants. As she puts it, she was lured to Islam because of the *purdah* and the security that it provided to women. According to her statement, "*Purdah* is the most wonderful dress for women in the world, and I have always loved to wear the *purdah*. It gives women a sense of security. Only Islam gives protection to women."[12]

Kamala Das, who was a rebel in her writing and beliefs and had exploded the hypocritical social life, again shocked her readers with her views. But, it would be imprudent to believe that her journey from Kamala Das to Kamala Suraiya was one of submission and surrender and that she would compromise on her viewpoint after her conversion.

Kamala Das or Kamala Suraiya, veiled or unveiled, Allah or Krishna, she always remained her own self, and she made this clear to her readers when she stated, "Religion cannot chain one's creativity. Islam is tolerant. Allah is the God of love and forgiveness. No religion can restrict me. I am always myself. I love being a Muslim now, and it does mean that I will always speak truth."[13] Very aptly said by Sreekumar Varma, in his tribute in the *Deccan Herald*, "When the soul ignites, words are often a balm. And from those words rise others with other words. Kamala Das inspired a young nation of poets. Her fiction too threw up several stark, aching moments."[14] This legacy of hers will go on and many new writers will be born who will carry on with their endeavours.

"Suraiya to Malayalee readers and Kamala Suraiya to the English-speaking world," as she had proclaimed after her conversion, undoubtedly was an iconoclast who courted controversies all through her career but was unquestionably a refreshing breath of air to the world of literature. She had said, "Allah will henceforth inspire my creativity whether it is poetry or paintings," and lived with this trust in Allah, till her last breath on 31 May 2009.

NOTES

1. K. Meera Bai, *Women's Voices* (New Delhi: Prestige, 1996) 137.
2. T.N. Geetha, "An Interview with Kamala Das," *Indian Women Novelists*, ed. R.K. Dhawan, Set 2, Vol II (New Delhi: Prestige, 1996), 87.
3. Gerda Lerner, The *Creation of Patriarchy* (New York: Oxford University Press, 1986) 229.
4. Helene Cixous, "The Laugh of the Medusa," trans. Keith Cohen and Paula Cohen, *New French Feminism*, ed. Elaine Marks (New York: Schockin, 1981) 312.
5. William Shakespeare, *Hamlet* (London: Cambridge University Press, 1950) Act II.
6. Marilyn Yalom, *Maternity, Morality and the Literature of Madness* (London: The Pennsylvania State University Press, 1985) 9.
7. Annis Pratt, *Archetypal Patterns in Women's Fiction* (Brighton: Harvester Press, 1982) 142-43.
8. Jean-Paul Sartre, *What is Literature*, trans. Bernard Frechtman (London: Methuen, 1950) 41.
9. Pam Morris, *Literature and Feminism: An Introduction* (Oxford: Blackwell, 1993) 7.
10. Sharad Rajimwale, "Kamala Das—Need for Re-assessment," *Kamala Das: A Critical Spectrum*, ed. Rajeshwar Mittapalli and Pier Piciucco (New Delhi: Atlantic, 2001) 163.
11. Mary Warnock, *Existentialism* (London: Oxford University Press, 1977) 55.
12. http://www.rediff.com/news/1999/dec/14kamala.htm
13. http http://www.rediff.com/news/1999/dec/14kamala.htm
14. http://www.deccanherald.com/content/6643/kamala-ignited-soul.html

Kamala Das: In Conversation with the Author

October 21, 1999

Talking to Kamala Das at length about her childhood, family, her passion for art and literature and her perspective, one gets a very clear insight about the genuine woman in her.

As a writer, poet and artist, Das constantly engaged herself in contemplating about the very intricate and subtle matters of human emotions, especially love, which she believed was the only ultimate truth. She was sensitive yet realistic about every aspect of womanhood—the female body, her mind and heart and used both literature and painting as a medium to portray not only its beauty but also its imperfections. She spoke about woman's weaknesses and strengths and without inhibitions discussed her own vulnerabilities, confines and hidden desires. Yet, neither she, nor her characters, ever surrendered to the subjugations of society, instead they firmly stood upright in their beliefs and perspective, and followed their own instincts. She dared to discuss all the unexplored thoughts and actions, which till her time, had not been aired by any woman writer. Her belief that every imperfection of the body, heart and mind is saleable, proved right looking at the popularity with which her autobiography *My Story* was received. The book got translated into more than a dozen languages.

Her blatant approach and absolute frankness to deal with dilemma with ease, gets depicted in all her works and this ability of Das helps her to arrest the attention of her readers. Her journey from Kamala Das to Kamala Suraiya, again proved that she was constantly in pursuit of self-discovery and contentment. The interview below provides her readers an opportunity to get a closer look at her thoughts and a better understanding of the writer herself.

SP: Do you remember how and when you started writing?

KD: I lived in an atmosphere where there were many writers around me. I grew up seeing and experiencing it. Personally I took to writing to gain the admiration of my father, to earn his love and appreciation. I used to always hear him praise my mother's literary works. In school, I wrote to impress my teachers and to beat the English students in their line. They used to consider us (Indian students) very inferior and secondary to them and by writing in their language I took my vengeance and beat them at their own game.

SP: Do you think it was your autobiography, *My Story*, that made you instantaneously popular to your English readers in India? What aspect or aspects of your autobiography do you think made it so popular?

KD: In our country every weakness is saleable. People in India are very keen to know about other people's private affairs. That is exactly why I think my books became an instant hit and people reacted so much. Pretentiousness is a very dominant behaviour among the general public here. People act as if they resent shady things like those mentioned in my book, but in the shadow of darkness all these events actually take place, don't they? The people, who break the rules and exploit women, are the very same people, who are responsible for our society's welfare and development. When people like me, reveal these acts to outer world, it upsets them, and they make a big hue and cry about the whole issue. I find this attitude very queer. I draw inspiration from my own experiences and things I witness around me. I have written the truth and I hate pretence. My writings are honest and my readers know it well. Outside India people have appreciated my work immensely. *My Story* has been translated in nearly thirteen languages across the world.

SP: You popularity was and still rests in your poems. What drove you to prose?

KD: Poetry comes to me naturally and is an expression of my deep emotions. In today's world these emotions don't suffice for your livelihood. Fiction gives me my source of income.

SP: How are your fictional works born?

KD: As I said, I took to fiction to survive. Moreover limiting myself to poetry, or for that matter any one specific thing is not my attitude. Life is a one time gift and I love to experiment and experience everything to its fullest in this short period. I write, paint, and read . . . you never know if you will be born human again to do all these things. So all our wishes should be fulfilled here, in this one lifetime. Variety is the spice of life—isn't it? My prose works are also very much a part of my own experiences in life.

SP: Man-woman relationship has been the most dealt with theme in your prose works. What is your perspective on this relationship, looking at the fact that women today have progressed and are more independent and prefer single life?

KD: I don't believe that marriage means just sexual union of two people for the lone purpose of procreation. Neither do I agree to a forceful and compelling marriage. Everyone thinks differently. Individuals, may it be men or women, should be given the freedom to voice their opinion and live in accordance to their own liking. Mental vibe is a very essential element in marriage and that I believe has nothing to do with the social status of the family. Frankly speaking, I personally believe in the sanctity of love; but sanctity of marriage—no. In India women are still apprehensive to voice their views, but things have changed a lot since my early days.

SP: Has your mother Balamani Amma's writings influenced you or your thoughts?

KD: No, I don't think she has influenced my writings. My mother was deeply influenced by theology and her works have theosophical ideas and views. I could never understand her writings. My thinking was quite different; I like the world, which is more human, and all-encompassing. I wanted to experience everything in life as an ordinary human being. My thoughts are reflected in what I write. I find it difficult to incorporate my mother's thoughts and views.

SP: Could you brief me about your childhood; did it influence your writing?

KD: I do not have any pleasant or exciting memories about my childhood. I think it was the distressing childhood that inspired me to write.

SP: What ultimate objectives do you look out for in your works? Is there a particular message you wish to convey or a definite purpose when you write a literary text?

KD: A piece of literary work is like a newborn baby just out of its mother's womb. Now what is the objective or purpose of this baby, one has to wait and watch. The mother can't guess. I consider my literary work similar to this. Once a literary piece is printed and published, it is an entity in itself and in the hands of the readers. It is time that shapes and decides its future. It may be accepted or rejected. The readers are the ones who ultimately decide its fate—they give it a purpose or direction, not the writer. I as a writer am only instrumental in its birth and my right ceases the moment its composition is over. The rest is left to the readers.

SP: What message would you like to give to the Indian womanhood?

KD: I have always wanted women to be self-sufficient. In India people are reluctant to give up their old beliefs and adapt to the new. The secondary status of woman should be altered and she should be given an independent identity and place in society. She too should make an effort to establish her own self and achieve a respectful position, for which I believe education and financial independence is a must.

Kamala Suraiya: In Conversation with the Author

July 3, 2001

SP: Last time when I met you in 1999, I was speaking to Kamala Das a staunch believer of Lord Krishna and here I am today speaking to Kamala Suraiya. What prompted this big change in your life?

KD: Though I have been a Hindu, I had been contemplating conversion since the 70s. At that stage my husband did not approve of it saying I was not mature enough to take the decision. Now that I am all alone and seek protection and love, I felt the time for making the change had arrived.

SP: What in Islam influenced you?

KD: As I said I am now all alone, and I feel very lonely. I need love, company and protection. I am now looking for security and comfort. I don't want to remain like an orphan, unclaimed and unattended. I have realized that there is no religion which safeguards and protects the women folk more than Islam. The Hindu society has always sneered at me, but Islam gave me friends who love and admire me. I feel honoured and protected under the umbrella of Islam.

SP: You were one of the foremost modern women writers in Indian literature who asserted for women's independence and freedom. What led you to this change in thinking?

KD: Every individual born likes and enjoys freedom. I am someone who enjoyed freedom in abundance, so much so that I felt being haunted by it. I had long desired for a master who can claim and possess me. Today I feel secure being owned by Allah. I am Allah's slave; Islam is now my protector and this is my new identity—Kamala Suraiya.

Religion and belief are matters of one's personal preference. This is man's fundamental right. I have only exercised my freedom by opting for a conversion.

SP: What can your readers and the literary world look forward to from the creative artist in you in future? Will this conversion affect the way Kamala Das used to write?

KD: This is a new life for me. My canvas won't have any more women portraits sketched on them; my literary work will be guided by Allah and I will be writing in praise of Allah. I am not a feminist, I am an ordinary woman. Islam teaches its followers to be honest, and I will continue to write honestly. Religion cannot change my writing.

SP: Kamala Das was the spokesperson of the Indian woman, what will be the future endeavours of Kamala Suraiya?

KD: I would like to work for the Hindu-Muslim harmony and write in praise of Allah. I would also like to do something for the less fortunate women and children of our society.

Bibliography

Primary Sources

Anand, Mulk Raj. *The Lost Child and Other Stories*. London: J.A. Allen, 1934.

_____. *The Barber's Trade Union and Other Stories*. London: Jonathan Cape, 1994.

_____. *Mulk Raj Anand: Selected Short Stories*, ed. M.K. Naik. New Delhi: Arnold Heinemann, 1997.

Austen, Jane. *Persuasion*. London: Oxford University Press, 1818.

Bhattacharya, Bhabani. *Steel Hawk and Other Stories*. Delhi: Hind Pocket Books, 1968.

Chatterjee, Santa and Seetha. *Tales of Bengal*. London: Oxford, 1992.

Das, Kamala. *My Story*. New Delhi: Sterling, 1988.

_____. *Alphabet of Lust*. New Delhi: Orient Paperback, 1976.

_____. *Padmavatim the Harlot and Other Stories*. New Delhi: Sterling Paperbacks, 1994.

_____. *Summer in Calcutta*. New Delhi: Everest Press, 1965.

_____. *The Sandal Trees and Other Stories*, trans. V.C. Harris and C.K. Mohammed Ummer. Hyderabad: Disha, 1995.

De, Shobha. *Socialite Evenings*. New Delhi: Penguin India, 1989.

Desai, Anita. *In Custody*. Harmondsworth, Middlesex: Penguin, 1985.

_____. *Clear Light of Day*. New York: Penguin, 1980.

_____. *Games at Twilight and Other Stories*. London: Heinemann, 1978.

Deshpande, Shashi. *That Long Silence*. New Delhi: Penguin, 1989.

_____. *The Dark Holds No Terrors*. New Delhi: Vikas, 1980.

_____. *A Matter of Time*. New Delhi: Penguin, 1996.

_____. *Roots and Shadows*. Hyderabad: Orient Longman, 1993.

_____. *The Binding Vine*. New Delhi: Vikas, 1980.

_____. *The Legacy and Other Stories*. Calcutta: Writers Workshop, 1978.

_____. *The Intrusion and Other Stories*. New Delhi: Penguin, 1993.
Hossain, Attia. *Phoenix Fled and Other Stories*. Calcutta: Rupa, 1993.
Iswaran, Manjeri S. *Naked Shingles*. Madras: Shaktikaryalayam, 1941.
_____. *Siva Ratri*. Madras: Shaktikaryalayam, 1943.
_____. *Angry Dust*. Madras: Shaktikaryalayam, 1944.
_____. *Rikshwallah*. Madras: Alliance, 1946.
_____. *Fancy Tales*. Madras: Shaktikaryalayam, 1947.
_____. *No Anklets for Her*. Madras: Mitra, 1949.
_____. *Immersion*. Madras: Shaktikaryalayam, 1951.
_____. *Painted Tigers*. Madras: Dhanus, 1956.
_____. *A Madras Admiral*. Madras: Dhanus, 1959.
Jhabvala, Ruth Prawer. *Like Birds. Like Fishes and Other Stories*. New York: Norton, 1964.
_____. *How I Became Holy Mother and Other Stories*. New York: Norton, 1964.
_____. *A Stronger Climate: Nine Short Stories*. London: John Murray, 1968.
_____. *An Expression of India*. London: John Murray, 1972.
_____. *Get Ready for Battle*. Harmondsworth: Penguin, 1981.
Markandaya, Kamala. *Nectar in a Sieve*. New York: Signet, 1961.
Mahadevan, Meera. *Shulamith*. New Delhi: Arnold-Heinemann, 1980.
Mehta, Dina. *And Some Take a Lover*. Delhi: Rupa, 1992.
_____. *The Other Woman and Short Stories*. New Delhi: Vikas, 1981.
Mukherjee, Bharati. *Darkness*. Canada: Penguin, 1985.
_____. *The Middleman and Other Stories*. New York: Groove Press, 1988.
Narayan, R.K. *Malgudi Days*. London: William Heinemann, 1982.
_____. *Dodu and Other Stories*. Mysore: Indian Thought Publications, 1943.
_____. *Cyclone and Other Stories*. Madras: Rock House Sons, 1944.
_____. *An Astrologer's Day and Other Stories*. London: Eyre and Spottiswoode, 1947.
_____. *Lawley Road*. Mysore: Indian Thought Publications, 1956.
_____. *Gods, Demons and Others*. New York: Viking, 1965.
_____. *A Horse and Two Goats*. New York: Viking, 1970.
_____. *Old and New*. Mysore: Indian Thought Publications, 1956.
Nehru, Jawaharlal. *The Discovery of India*. New Delhi: Jawaharlal Nehru Memorial Fund, 1981.

Nimbkar, Jai. *Temporary Answers*. New Delhi: Orient Longman, 1974.
Rao, Raja. *The Cow of the Barricades and Other Stories*. London: Oxford, 1947.
_____. *The Policeman and the Rose*. Delhi: Oxford, 1978.
Roy, Arundhati. *The God of Small Things*. New Delhi: IndiaInk, 1997.
Sahgal, Nayantara. *Rich Like Us*. London: Sceptre, 1983.
_____. *Mistaken Identity*. New York: New Directions, 1988.
Shakespeare, William. *Antony and Cleopatra*. London: Cambridge University Press, 1950.

Secondary Sources

Abhedanenda, Swami. *India and Her People*. 1906; Kessinger, 1998.
Abrams, M.H. *A Glossary of Literary Terms*. New York: Macmillan, 1941.
Altekar, A.S. *The Position of Woman in Indian Civilization: From Prehistoric Times to the Present Day*. New Delhi: Motilal Banarasi Dass, 1959.
Amur, G.S. *The Legacy and Other Stories*. Calcutta: Writers Workshop, 1978.
Anne, McClintlock. *Imperial Leather: Race, Gender, and Sexuality in the Colonial Context*. New York: Routledge, 1995.
Bai, Meera K. *Women's Voices*. New Delhi: Prestige, 1996.
Basham, A.L. *The Wonder that was India*. New York: Grove, 1954.
Bates, H.E. *The Modern Short Stories: A Critical Survey*. London: Macmillan, 1941.
Beauvoir, Simone de. *The Second Sex*. London: Penguin, 1953.
Bharat-Aranyaka Upanishad. Calcutta: Modern Art Press, 1950.
Bhagavad-Gita As it Is. Bombay: The Bhaktivendanta Book Trust, 1986.
Bhatt, Yashoda, ed. *The Image of Woman in Indian Literature*. New Delhi: B.R., 1993.
Butler, Judith. *Gender Trouble: Feminism and Subversion of Identity*. New York: Routledge, 1990.
Chopin, Kate. *The Awakening*. 1899; rpt. New York: Bantam, 1988.
Connor, O'Frank. *The Lonely Voice: A Study of the Short Stories*. London: Macmillan, 1965.
Conard, Joseph. *Notes on Life and Letters*. London: Putnam, 1921.

Cixous, Helene. "The Laugh of Medusa," trans. Keith Cohen & Paul Cohen, *New French Feminism*, ed. Elaine Max. New York: Schockin, 1981.

Cowasjee, Saros. *Mulk Raj Anand and His Critics*. The Banasthali Patrika, Jan. 1969.

Das, Veena Noble, ed. *Feminism and Literature*. New Delhi: Prestige, 1995.

Das, Veena Noble and R.K. Dhawan. *Fiction of Nineties*. New Delhi: Prestige Books, 1994.

Desai, Neeraja and Meithereyi Krishnaraj. *Women and Society in India*. Delhi: Ajanta, 1987.

Dhawan, R.K., ed. *Indian Women Novelists*. 18 vols. New Delhi: Prestige, 1991, 1993, 1995.

Durant, Will. *Story of Civilization: Our Oriental Heritage*. M.F.J Books, 1935.

Dwivedi, A.N. *Study in Contemporary Indian-English Short Stories*. New Delhi: B.R., 1991.

Eagleton, Mary, ed. *Feminist Literary Theory: A Reader*. Oxford: Blackwell, 1996.

Encyclopedia Britannica. London: Encyclopedia Britannica Inc., 1997.

Ferguson, Mary Ann, Comp. *Images of Women in Literature*. Boston: Houghton, Miffin, 1973.

Firestone, Shulamith. *The Dialectic of Sex*. New York: Bantam, 1971.

Foster, E.M. *Aspects of Novel*. London: Edward Arnold, 1960.

Freud, Sigmund. *Introduction to Lectures on Psycho-Analysis,* trans. Rivjere. London: George Allen & Unwin, 1949.

Friedan, Betty. *The Feminine Mystique*, 1963. Harmondsworth: Penguin, 1986.

Frost, Robert. *Collected Poems, Prose and Plays*. New York: Library of America, 1995.

Gallop, Jane. *Around 1981*. New York: Routledge, 1991.

_____. *Feminism and Psycho-Analysis: The Daughters' Seduction*. London: Macmillan, 1982.

Gidwani, Bhawan S. *The Return of Aryans*. New Delhi: Penguin, 1994.

Hales, Dianne. *Just Like a Woman*. New York: Bantam, 1999.

Horowitz, E.A. *A Short History of Indian Literature*. London: Rare, 1973.

Hudson, W.H. *An Introduction to the Study of English Literature*. London: George G. Harrap, 1913.

Iyengar, K.R. Srinivasa. *Indian Writing in English*, 4th Ed. New Delhi: Sterling, 1984.

_____. *Introduction to the Study of English Literature*. New Delhi: Sterling, 1987.

Jacobson, Dornne & Susan S. Wadley. *Women in India*. New Delhi: Manohar, 1986.

Jacobus, Mary ed. *Women Writing and Writing about Women*. London: Croom Helm, 1979.

Jain, Dewaki. *Indian Woman*. Delhi: Publication Division, 1976.

Janapathi, Varalakshmi. *Indian Woman through Ages*. New Delhi, 2002.

Jardine, Alice. *Genisis: Configuration of Women and Modernity*. Ithaca: Cornell University Press, 1985.

Jordan, Ellen "The Christening of the New Woman," *The Victorian Newsletter*, Spring, 1995.

Jung, Anees. *Unveiling India: A Woman's Journey*. New Delhi: Penguin, 1988.

Karkala, John B. Alphonso. *Indo-English Literature in the Nineteenth Century*. Mysore: University of Mysore, 1970.

Kaur, Iqbal, ed. *Perspectives on Kamala Das's Prose*. New Delhi: Intellectual, 1995.

Kohli, Devindra. *Kamala Das*. New Delhi: Arnold-Heinemann, 1975.

Krishnaswamy, Shanta. *The Woman in Indian Fiction in English*. New Delhi: Ashish, 1984.

Lerner, Gerda. *The Creation of Patriarchy*. London: Oxford University Press, 1986.

Litz, A. Walton. Ed. *Major American Short Stories*. Bombay: Allied, 1975.

Lubbock, Percy. *The Craft of Fiction*. London: Jonathan Cape, 1954.

Manohar, Murali D. *Kamala Das: Treatment of Love in Her Poetry*. Gulbarga: JIWE, 1999.

Marshal, Richard. *Great Events of the Twentieth Century: How They Changed Our Lives*. New York: Dainippon, 1977.

Melwani, M.D. *Themes in Indo-Anglican Literature*, 2nd ed. Bareilly: Prakash, 1977.

Merson, A.J. *Modern Short Stories*. Bombay: Macmillan India, 1981.

Mill, John Stuart. *The Subjection of Women* (1869). Rep. *Three Essays by J.S. Mill*, World Classics Series. London: Oxford University Press, 1996.

Millett, Kate. *Sexual Politics*. London: ABACUS, 1972.

Mitchell, Juliet. "Feminity, Narrative and Psychoanalysis," *Women: The Longest Revolution.* London: Penguin, 1984.

_____. *Psycho-Analysis and Feminism*. Harmondsworth: Penguin, 1975.

Mittapalli, Rajeshwar and Pier Piciucco, ed. *Kamala Das: A Critical Spectrum*. New Delhi: Atlantic, 2001.

Moi, Toril. *Sexual/Textual Politics: Feminist Literary Theory*. London: Methuen, 1985.

Morris, Pam. *Literature and Feminism: An Introduction*. Oxford: Blackwell, 1993.

Mukherjee, Meenakshi. *The Twice Born Fiction: Themes and Techniques of the Indian Novel in English*. New Delhi: Arnold Heinemann, 1974.

Naik, M.K. *A History of Indian English Literature*. Sahitya Akademi. 1982.

_____. ed. *Perspectives on Indian Fiction in English*. New Delhi: Abhinav, 1985.

Narayan, R.K. *Reluctant Guru*. Delhi: Hindi Pocket Books, 1974.

Pathak, R.S. *Introduction to Recent Indian Fiction*. New Delhi: Prestige, 1994.

Paul Sartre, Gene. *What is Literature*, trans. Bernard Frenchtman. London: Methuen, 1950.

_____. *Existential Psycho-Analysis*. New York: Philosophy Library, 1955.

_____. *Saint Genet: Actor and Martyr*, trans. from French by Bernard Frenchtman. New York: Mentor, 1963.

Poe, Edgar Allan. "Twice-Told Tales by Nathaniel Hawthorne: A Review," *American Literature Survey*, Vol. II, ed. Milton R. Stern. New York: The Viking Press, 1969.

Pratt, Annis. *Archetypal Patterns in Women's Fiction*. Brighton: Harvester Press, 1982.

Rajeshekhar, *Kavyameemansa* Trans. Kedarnath Sharma. Patna: Bihar Rashtra Bhasha Parishad, 1965.

Rajgopalachari, C., trans., *Mahabharata*. Bombay: Bharatiya Vidya Bhavan, 1951.

Ramamurti, K.S. *Rise of the Novel in English*. New Delhi: Sterling, 1987.

Ram, Atma. "Interviews with Indo-English Writers." Calcutta: Writers Workshop, 1983.

Rao, C.R.Visweswara. *Indian Writing Today*. New Delhi: Prestige, 1996.

Reddy, P. Bayapa. *Studies in Indian Writing in English*. New Delhi: Prestige, 1990.

Rao, Yamuna Raja, ed. *The Images of Indian in Indo-Anglican Literature*. New Delhi: Creative, 1994.

Reid, Ian. *The Short Story*. London: Methuen, 1977.

Sandhu, Sarabjit K. *The Image of Woman in the Novels of Shashi Deshpande*. New Delhi: Prestige, 1991.

Sengupta, Padmini. *Everyday Life in Ancient India*. New York: Oxford University Press, 1950.

Shastry, Shakuntala Rao. *Women in the Sacred Laws*. Bombay: Bharatiya Vidya Bhavan, 1959.

_____. *Woman in the Vedic Age*. Bombay: Bharatiya Vidya Bhavan, 1959.

Shirwadkar, Meena. *Images of Women in the Indo-Anglican Novel*. New Delhi: Sterling, 1979.

Showalter, Elaine, ed. *The New Feminist Criticism: Essays on Women, Literature and Theory*. New York: Pantheon, 1985

_____. "Towards a Feminist Poetic," *Women's Writing and Writing about Women*, ed. Mary Jacobus. London: Croom Helm, 1979.

Singh, Sushila, ed. *Feminism and Recent Fiction in English*. New Delhi: Prestige, 1991.

Spacks, Patricia Mayer. *The Female Imagination*. London: Allen and Unwin, 1976.

Spencer, Dorothy. *Indian Fiction in English*. Philadelphia: University of Pennsylvania Press, 1960.

Tharu, Susie and K. Lalitha, ed. *Women Writing in India*, Vol. I, O.U.P., 1991.

Venugopal, C.V. *The Indian Short Story in English--A Survey*. Bareilly: Prakash, 1976.

Verghese, Paul. *Essays on Indian Writing in English*. New Delhi: N.V., 1975.

_____. *Problems of the Indian Creative Writers in English*. Bombay: Somaiya, 1971.

Vivekananda, Swami. *Our Women*. Calcutta: Advaita Ashram, 1982.

Warnock, Mary. *Existentialism*. London: Oxford University Press, 1977.

Williams, H.M. *Indo-Anglican Literature 1800-1970*. Madras: Orient Longman, 1976.

William, Raymond. *The Long Revolution*. 1961; Harmondsworth: Penguin, 1965.

Wolf, Naomi. *Fire with Fire: The New Female Power and How it Will Change the 21st Century*. Chatto and Windus: London, 1993.

Woolf, Virginia. *A Room of One's Own*. 1928. Harmondsworth: Penguin, 1967.

_____. "Professions for Women," *Feminist Literary Theory: A Reader*, ed. Mary Eagleton. Oxford: Blackwell, 1996.

Yalom, Marilyn. *Maternity, Morality and the Literature of Madness*. London: The Pennsylvania State University Press, 1985.

Research Work on Kamala Das

Kalithasan, N. *Kamala Das: A Critical Study*. Madurai, 1990.

Kameshwara Rao, R. *The Making of the Self: A Study of Kamala Das's Poems*. Krishna Devaraya, 1990.

Raveendran, N.V. *Poetry of Kamala Das: A Stylistic Study*. Calicut, 199.

Dwadashiwar, Jaya Suresh. *Quest for Identity: A Thematic Study of the Poetry of Kamala Das*. Nagpur, 1991.

Geetha Kumari, B.R. *The Evaluation of the Self in the Poetry of Kamala Das*. Calicut, 1993.

Radha, P.S. *A Comparative Study of the Ideas of Womanhood in the Poems of Kamala Das and Balamaniamma*. Calicut, 1997.

Kumar, Rajesh. *Kamala Das's Work: A Feminist Perspective*. Punjab, 1998.